How to Split up – and Survive Financially

TONY HETHERINGTON

London
UNWIN PAPERBACKS
Boston   Sydney

First published by Unwin Paperbacks 1986

UNWIN® PAPERBACKS
40 Museum Street, London WC1A 1LU, UK

Unwin Paperbacks
Park Lane, Hemel Hempstead, Herts HP2 4TE, UK

George Allen & Unwin Australia Pty Ltd
8 Napier Street, North Sydney, NSW 2060, Australia

Unwin Paperbacks with the
Port Nicholson Press
PO Box 11–838 Wellington, New Zealand

E00001C7139

British Library Cataloguing in Publication Data

Hetherington, Tony
    How to split up and survive financially.
1. Separate maintenance—England
2. Divorce—England
I. Title
344.2061'66   KD769
ISBN 0−04−332120−8
ISBN 0−04−332121−6 Pbk

Set in 10 on 11 point Palatino by Bedford Typesetters Ltd, Bedford,
and printed in Great Britain by Cox & Wyman Limited, Reading.

Contents

England and Wales have a different legal system from that of Scotland. The advice in this book is based on the laws of England and Wales, although many of the points made – particularly on the tax and benefit rules – apply equally in all three countries. In many sections notes have been added highlighting the different position in Scotland.

1

Pounds, Pence and Parting

*Marriage makes an end of many short follies –
being one long stupidity.*

Friedrich Nietzsche (1844–1900)

Untying the Knot
Getting a divorce is almost as easy as getting married, and nearly as commonplace. In 1984 there were something like 350,000 weddings in Britain – and 178,940 divorce petitions were filed. Since 1980 more than 1 million people have become divorcees. By 1990 that figure will have reached 3 million.

Easy divorce is a modern idea. Until 1857 getting a divorce meant you had to get a special Act of Parliament. As recently as the 1960s you still had to prove your spouse was guilty of a 'matrimonial offence'. Divorce court tales of cruelty, adultery and desertion provided many juicy headlines for the Sunday papers.

Now, divorce could hardly be easier. You can even do it by post. To be single again, all you need do is prove that your marriage has irretrievably broken down by showing any of these circumstances apply to you:

* your spouse has committed adultery and you find it intolerable to go on living together;

* your spouse has behaved so badly you can no longer be expected to go on living together;

* your spouse has deserted you for a period of at least two years;

* you have been living apart for at least two years and your spouse agrees to the divorce;

* you have been living apart for at least five years – in which case you can have your divorce whether your other half likes it or not!

To apply for a divorce in England and Wales you must have been married for at least a year (it was two years until 1984). In Scotland there is no minimum period of marriage; you can go straight from the altar to the courtroom if you like.

Whether you like it or not, one spouse has to ask for the divorce, perhaps exposing himself or herself to family accusations of having been to blame for ending the marriage. A committee set up by the Lord Chancellor has recommended (August 1985) a change to allow a couple to file a *joint* petition for divorce.

When the petitioner (that's the spouse who wants the divorce) asks the county court to end his or her marriage, the application form that has to be completed provides spaces for financial claims to be made at the same time.

Even if you don't seriously plan to press a financial claim, behave as though you do. It's easier than re-opening the matter at a later stage.

The divorce petition, including details of any financial claims, is sent by the court to the respondent (that's the spouse who's being divorced). The respondent has to reply to the court, confirming receipt of the petition and saying whether the action will be defended.

Assuming the respondent doesn't want to fight the case, the next step is for the petitioner to ask the court to proceed, and at this point the court will need a sworn statement providing details of the two-year separation, the adultery, or whatever other reason has been given for wanting the divorce in the first place.

Financial claims take a back seat at this stage, unless one of the parties has lodged a claim for what's called **maintenance pending suit.** This is a request for interim payments to last until the full financial arrangements are dealt with, and such claims are processed very quickly, without pre-judging either the divorce itself or the rightness of the long-term claim for money or property.

With maintenance and similar claims left to one side, the court will consider the divorce petition and the evidence offered in support of it. If all is well, the judge will grant a *decree nisi*, and six weeks later the petitioner can ask for this to be made into a *decree absolute*, bringing the marriage to an end.

In Scotland, where the petitioner is called the *pursuer* and the respondent is known as the *defender*, it can all happen much more quickly. There is no *decree nisi* – the marriage is ended at a stroke, though either spouse can lodge an appeal against the divorce within 21 days.

Only one divorce in about 50 is now defended. The arguments these days are rarely over who did what to whom (or with whom). The new battleground is a financial one. The tools of war are the affidavit of means, the bank statement, the property deed and the tax return. There are few winners. Just good losers and bad losers. And knowing the rules of the game before you play it can make all the difference.

Long-term Finances – Who Can Ask for What, from Whom, and How

Who?
Although legally a husband can demand financial support from his wife, it's very rare for this to happen. (A recent case was in January 1985, when Barnsley County Court ordered the estranged wife of a striking miner to pay him £12 a week while the miners' strike continued.) So let's assume payments are always made by a husband and received by his wife and children, because that's what the real world is like.

What?
The courts are amazingly powerful in sorting out who gets what when a couple split up. The most common requests they get are for:

£   maintenance for a wife and/or children (see Chapter 2);

£   the transfer of the family home to the wife (whether owned or tenanted), or its sale so she can take her share in cash (see Chapter 6);

£   a lump sum (known as a capital payment in Scotland) reflecting the wife's share of the couple's savings and other assets (see Chapter 7).

The courts also have the power to order a husband to:

£   set up a trust fund for the benefit of his wife and children;

£   sign over his life insurance policies;

£   pay compensation to his wife for the loss of any pension she would have received from his employers if the marriage had continued.

How much?

How much a court will award in maintenance or other financial provision is completely up to the judge. There is no law telling him (or her) what to do.

Until 1984 courts were supposed to try to put the couple in the same position financially as they would have been if the marriage had not ended. This was totally unrealistic, and anyone who believes two individuals can live as cheaply as one couple has clearly never been involved in a divorce.

NEW GUIDELINES

Now under the Matrimonial and Family Proceedings Act, courts have been given two major guidelines:

* The children take priority, and the court has to consider their welfare first when sorting out financial matters.

* The husband and wife should – if possible – aim to become financially independent of one another, ending claims that an ex-wife can have 'a meal ticket for life'. The target now is a 'clean break' – and the courts can order exactly that, either immediately or by granting a maintenance order for a limited number of years instead of an indefinite period.

In Scotland the 'clean break' legislation is called the Family Law (Scotland) Act, 1985, notwithstanding that, although it was approved by Parliament in that year, it has had to await the fixing of a date by the Secretary of State for Scotland before coming into effect.

There is a third guideline too:

In recent years courts have rarely taken a husband's or wife's conduct into account in deciding who gets what. Now, the courts can listen to tales of matrimonial nastiness if, in the words of the new rules, 'it would be inequitable to disregard' them.

In Scotland the courts never stopped listening to

such tales, so now the two legal systems are the same again.

THE CLEAN BREAK

The significance of the Matrimonial and Family Proceedings Act in bringing about the much-vaunted clean break between husband and wife was hugely exaggerated while the proposed law was before Parliament.

Since it came into force in October 1984 the dissenting voices seem to have been stilled, probably because it has become pretty clear that the wife with children of school age, and the middle-aged or elderly wife, are unlikely to be affected. Young wives, or those with jobs or the ability to get them, do not attract as much sympathy and will be encouraged to be, or become, self-sufficient.

Potentially at least, the biggest change in the 1984 Act is that it allows courts to *order* a clean break, with just a division of capital and no continuing maintenance, or, perhaps, a limited amount of maintenance for a short period while a wife gets used to being an ex-wife and finds her own financial feet. Previously a wife was entitled to refuse an offer, however generous, that involved giving up her right to ask for more in future years.

Whether the courts will make extensive use of their new power is another matter. So far, there is little sign that they will.

From whom?

So who does an aggrieved wife go to with her claim for financial support? The magistrates' courts, the county courts and the High Court all have certain powers.

Magistrates are useful for urgent cases of financial need – but they can't give you a divorce, nor can they order a property transfer, nor can they award you a lump sum of more than £500. They have some interesting powers to enforce court orders, but that's *after* you've already won your maintenance order.

The High Court (in Scotland, the Court of Session in Edinburgh) generally means High Expense. For practical purposes, forget it unless your solicitor advises otherwise. Its main function in the wake of the 1984 legislation will probably be to sort out knottier contested divorces.

It is the county courts (or in Scotland the Sheriff Courts) that make up the backbone of the system, in terms of both making financial orders and granting divorces themselves. Not all county courts handle divorce work though, so if you plan to get involved in the paperwork yourself, give your local branch of the county court a ring to find out whether they are also a divorce court; it could save you time or a wasted journey.

How?

Whether you are the partner asking the county court for a divorce or the one being divorced, if you want to claim financial support you should include with your divorce petition what is quaintly referred to as a **Prayer for Financial Relief,** which means you should ask for money. The court will provide a form asking what sort of financial help you want. What you *don't* have to do, perhaps surprisingly, is tell the court exactly how much you are asking for. The court will make up its own mind without prompting.

Before the court makes any financial order both sides have to submit sworn statements (affidavits) giving all the information a judge will need to help him make up his mind. If you are asking for an order involving your home, you have to submit your affidavit explaining why you are asking for whatever it is you want with your application. A copy is then sent to your other half for his or her comments. If you are only asking for money, no affidavit is needed yet. First, your spouse is asked for his or her affidavit giving full details of all savings and income. These details have to be submitted to the court within 14 days from the service of your application on your spouse. Then, a copy of the affidavit is sent to you, and you are given 14 days to provide identical details. Again, the court will give your spouse a copy of whatever you say about your own finances.

Your solicitor will prepare your affidavit for you of course, but it does no harm at all to know how the system works, so you may find it educative to have a look at form D635, which you can get from the court. This itemises the sort of information the court thinks matters. For example:

* how long the marriage lasted;

* who paid for the matrimonial home or other expensive items;

* in whose name property is registered;

* how much you have in either earnings or income from investments – including amounts you could reasonably expect to earn if you chose to apply yourself;

* how much you reckon you need to live on;

* what savings you have;

* how old you are;

* how old your children are.

You will almost certainly use this form of affidavit if you are handling your own case, but if you really are involved in a financial fight with your spouse, doing it yourself is a rotten way to save money. Avoiding a solicitor's bill in these circumstances is perfectly legal – but so is taking out your own appendix. That doesn't make it a sensible thing to do though.

TRUTH OR CONSEQUENCES
Suppose you read your spouse's financial affidavit with a growing sense of disbelief? You are sure there ought to be more money than that laying about somewhere, but where?

What you need is the procedure called **Discovery and Inspection.** An order for discovery means one side has to give the other a complete list of all the documents they have, or have had, which are relevant to the application for maintenance, or whatever. This would include bank statements, for example. Inspection means just that: you have to let the other side look at the documents.

Failing to tell the truth in an affidavit is serious stuff. In fact, it's perjury. However, even when faced with the most obvious lies, courts rarely do anything about it apart, perhaps, from subjecting the liar to a few barbed comments. So, don't take anything as gospel just because it's in an affidavit. It ain't necessarily so!

Foreign Policy

Getting a divorce and an order for financial support when you and your spouse are both living in this country can be as easy as falling off a log compared to the problems you may run into if your other half takes off abroad.

Since September 1985, though, things have become a bit easier. Anyone living in the United Kingdom who is divorced or legally separated under a ruling of a foreign court can now go to a British court for a maintenance or property order – previously this was impossible.

This will mostly help immigrant wives whose husbands return to their former home country and divorce them.

2

Maintenance – Getting It, Keeping It, Changing It

In a divorce or separation the fortunate wife is the one who is financially independent. But for many wives – particularly those with children – there is no practical alternative to lodging a claim for financial support. Reaching a permanent agreement over maintenance payments can take years, and if there were no stop-gap provision then the less well-off wife could have a pretty miserable time of it.

As soon as divorce proceedings have been filed, you can apply both for **maintenance pending suit** and for **periodical payments.** It doesn't make an atom of difference whether you are the spouse being divorced or doing the divorcing. Maintenance pending suit is the name given to temporary payments ordered by the court to cover the period from separation to the making of a final order. It often used to be called alimony. Periodical payments is the name given to money due under the permanent order that will replace maintenance pending suit as soon as your marriage is ended. You can also ask for payments for the support of your children (called **aliment** in Scotland).

Maintenance Pending Suit

The court's decision on an application for maintenance pending suit is made fairly quickly at a private hearing at which both you and your spouse may be asked questions. The decision will be made at the end of the hearing.

The court will consider the finances of both husband and wife, including their sources of income and the expenses they face, such as rent or mortgage payments, food, clothing, and so on. There is no fixed formula for working out how much should be awarded as maintenance; the only rule is that the court has to be 'reasonable'. Often, this means maintenance pending suit is less than the amount of the final order. Courts tend to feel it is easier to backdate an increase later than to make a cut in payments – though husbands may not agree with this view.

An even more temporary sort of payment can be ordered if the court decides it doesn't even have enough information to make an order for maintenance pending suit. Then, the order will be for **interim maintenance pending suit** – not a very imaginative title, but the name does say it all.

The Final Maintenance Order

The longer-term periodical payments normally involve two hearings. There is a brief one at which the court decides whether it needs any more documentary evidence like wage slips and bank statements, followed by the actual hearing of the maintenance application. However, if both sides have reached an agreement on how much maintenance should be paid then they can ask the court to rubber-stamp it at the first hearing. This is called a **consent order**.

The wife

The nearest the system has come to any rule on maintenance for a spouse is the **'one-third'** principle. Under this, the court adds together the incomes – or likely incomes – of both husband and wife and then makes an order which tops up the wife's income so she gets one-third of the total.

For example
If John Smith earns £12,000 a year, and Jenny Smith earns – or could earn – £3,000 a year, that gives them a joint income of £15,000. A third of this is £5,000 – but Jenny only has £3,000 of her own, so John is ordered to pay her £2,000 a year to bring her income up to the one-third mark.

The use of one-third of joint incomes as a basis for maintenance goes back to the old ecclesiastical courts, but in modern times it was reaffirmed in 1973. Then, Lord Denning, in an Appeal Court decision, awarded a Mrs Wachtel £1,500 a year, on the basis that her husband earned £6,000 and she could herself bring in £750.

It can't be emphasised strongly enough that this is only a guideline. It does not include maintenance for children of the marriage, and it does not take into account any accompanying lump-sum or property order. Nor does it take into account the fairly recent 'clean-break' principle. It can really only be applied with fairness nowadays when the marriage has lasted some years, where the problems of a future home for the wife are sorted out separately – probably by a lump-sum award or property order – and where the picture is not distorted by the 'blameworthy' conduct of one party or the other.

The children
As with orders for maintenance between spouses, the courts can do pretty much what they like in ordering financial provision for a child.

A typical order for a child at primary school, whose father earns, say, £200 a week, would be around the £13 a week level. A child between 11 and 15 might get about £23, and a 16 or 17 year old £29 or £30. These are only examples though, and actual court awards vary hugely, depending on such things as the number of children in the family.

Normally, it is husbands who are ordered to pay for the support of their children, the money going to the wife or ex-wife. However, wives off-loading their children onto others – the children's grandparents, for instance – should not expect to escape their responsibilities; they can be ordered to pay maintenance to whoever actually has the children in their custody.

You Don't Have to Be Divorced

You don't have to be divorced to win maintenance, or be ordered to pay it. There doesn't even have to be a court order if both parties are content without it. The half-way houses on the road to divorce are **judicial separation** and just plain **separation,** and the substitutes for maintenance under a court order are **voluntary payments** and **payments under deed.**

Judicial separation

If you'd like all the advantages of being divorced but have a religious or other objection to divorce itself, this is for you. A judicial separation removes your legal duty to carry on living with your spouse. You'll have to give a court the same sort of evidence as if you were asking for a divorce, but at the end of the case you will not actually be divorced – and that means that neither party to a judicial separation becomes free to marry again. You need a real divorce for that.

What you do get out of a judicial separation is the chance to apply for exactly the same financial provision as in a proper divorce. And if you decide later that you do want a divorce, you don't need to produce further evidence on top of the case you already made for a judicial separation.

A judicial separation comes into effect as soon as it is granted – there is no *decree nisi* or *decree absolute*. It can be a useful course of action for an elderly wife who has no intention of remarrying, as it preserves her right to a widow's pension when her husband dies.

Informal separation

This is where a couple simply split up, without benefit of judges, magistrates, or other legal personnel. Legally, of course, you are still married and you still have all the mutual duties and responsibilities of a married couple.

In particular, the husband still has the common law duty to maintain his wife. If he doesn't do so by voluntary payments (and there may well be excellent tax reasons for rejecting this as an acceptable course of action) then the wife can sue for maintenance. It may be easier to suggest a deed of separation, particularly if there are no children.

Voluntary payments

The only immediately apparent advantage in a husband and wife reaching a private agreement over maintenance payments is that it does the lawyers out of their fees, though this may be a case of losing value in order to save on price. Voluntary payments do have the bonus of being tax free in the hands of the recipient, but the sting-in-the-tail catches the maker of the payments, who has to pay tax on all his income, even the slice he instantly gives away to his wife.

It is true that the husband may carry on being granted the married man's tax allowance, even though he is separated. Strictly, to get the allowance a husband has to live with or *wholly* maintain his wife, but the Inland Revenue Department has decided it will be liberal in interpreting the word 'wholly', so a man making voluntary payments to support his wife will get the tax relief even if she has some lesser amount of income from another source.

Whether this allowance is worth having is another matter. For the 1986–87 financial year the difference between the single person's tax allowance and the relief given to a married man is just £1,320. It is doubtful that any wife, let alone a tax inspector, would believe that £1,320 is enough to live on, so any husband who thinks voluntary payments are a good thing should think again.

If he is paying £1,320 or less it is unlikely he will get tax relief as a married man, and if he is paying more than this then he won't get relief because the payments are voluntary!

From the wife's point of view too, voluntary payments are a risky business. After all, a verbal contract isn't worth the paper it's written on, so 'voluntary' could easily mean 'might cease tomorrow'. Hardly a firm foundation on which to plan for the future.

Deed of separation
This is what to use if you have a lingering hope that your marriage may not have broken down completely. If you harbour thoughts of getting back together again, a deed of separation, privately agreed without judges or magistrates, will set down in writing the ground rules covering – amongst such things as arrangements for the children – precisely who pays what to whom, and how often.

It is legally enforceable, so any husband who thinks that avoiding having a court order made against him will help him get away without paying should forget this notion now. The advantage of a deed is its privacy: no court, no evidence, less stress.

It is true that you can have an oral agreement which, technically, is just as legally binding as a written one. However, this is an invitation to a major row later over who promised exactly what, and the Inland Revenue won't accept it anyway unless you both write the terms down and sign them, so why bother?

Payments under a deed of separation qualify for tax relief for the person making them; the other side of the coin is that the person receiving them has to pay tax, assuming the income is above their personal tax threshold. A husband making such payments can't also claim the married man's tax allowance – you can't have it both ways.

The exact wording of the deed is crucial as you have to make clear how much you actually intend to part with. This phrasing works:

'. . . agree to pay such a sum as after deduction of income tax at the basic rate for the time being in force shall leave £xxx per annum.'

If, for example, the husband agreed to pay £5,000 under this form of agreement, what he would actually be promising to pay is £7,042.25 less tax at 29 per cent. He would hand over the £5,000, keeping the balance as his tax relief. The wife would show on her tax return that she had received an income of £7,042.25 which had already been taxed at source.

Remember!
☞ Although a father can write separation deeds to cover any payments he makes to support his children, he *won't* get tax relief on those payments. Unlike payments to a wife, payments to children, or for their benefit, count for tax relief only if they are made under a court order. Arranging payments to children by private deed is about as efficient as pouring hot water into a chocolate teapot.

The Magistrates' Court
Magistrates' courts are essentially criminal courts, dealing with minor offences and the initial hearings for more serious crimes. Magistrates can't give anyone a divorce – but they do have the power to make financial orders.

You should not go to the magistrates if you have already started a divorce action in a different court, but as long as no divorce proceedings have been started – either by you or against you – you can turn to the magistrates for help if any of the following conditions apply to you:

* your husband has deserted you;

* your husband has behaved in such a way that you can't reasonably be expected to carry on living with him;

* your husband has failed to maintain you and/or your children.

You can also use the magistrates' court to rubber-stamp existing, informal maintenance arrangements.

If you and your husband have reached a private agreement over maintenance, the magistrates will turn it into a legally binding order.

Even if you haven't reached an agreement, a wife who has been living apart from her husband for at least three months, and receiving some payments from him, can ask the magistrates to grant an order turning those voluntary payments into a legal obligation. Husbands might like to avoid being over-generous in terms of voluntary payments for fear of finding themselves landed with an order set at a level they had no real intention of sticking to indefinitely!

Finding the right magistrates
You have a choice of magistrates to whom you can apply for maintenance:

● the court for the area where you live;

● the court for the area where your spouse lives;

● the court for the area where you last lived together.

How long will it take?
This depends on how busy the courts are. If the choices listed above give you two or three options, give them a ring and find out the size of their backlog.

Typically, you will get a hearing about six weeks after you put in your application. If this sort of delay would cause hardship, you can ask for an **expedited hearing** – that is, an urgent one – or for an interim order until the full case comes up.

What actually happens?
Magistrates' courts are about the easiest, quickest and

least expensive courts to deal with. You can just walk up to the enquiry counter and obtain a simple form to complete asking for financial support.

If the magistrate is happy that the information given shows – on the face of it – good reason for awarding maintenance, then a summons will be issued setting a date for the hearing.

The case is heard in private, with both sides giving evidence. If the magistrates are satisfied an award should be made, they will grant an order for a sum, which they fix, stating how often payments are to be made. They can also award a lump sum of up to £500 – for bigger lump sums you have to go to a higher court.

This maintenance order will self-destruct . . .
A maintenance order from the magistrates is not a divorce or a judicial separation. You can even ask for an order without being separated – for example, in cases where a husband neglects to maintain his wife.

But if a couple carry on living together for more than six months after the order is made then it automatically ceases to apply. In the same way, if you applied for maintenance because you were separated, and then you start living with your husband again, after six months the maintenance order self-destructs.

And if the order is of the rubber-stamp variety, with the couple having split up by consent and the husband having made voluntary payments that were then turned into a magistrates' order, getting together again has immediate results. As soon as you live together again the order is scrapped, with no six months' waiting period.

Going the whole hog later on . . .
Magistrates can grant you maintenance but they can't give you a divorce, so what happens if you win a maintenance order from the magistrates and then go to a higher court later on for the divorce itself?

The first thing to realise is that, on its own, this won't cancel the order made by the magistrates. For this to happen, the divorce court must itself make an order to take the place of the one granted by the magistrates.

If you have a magistrates' court order and subsequently win a divorce in another court, but don't ask for a new maintenance order, then the magistrates' order not only stays in force but to get any variation of it – up or down – you have to go back to the magistrates' court and not the divorce court.

Why bother with the magistrates?
Given that magistrates' powers are limited, why bother with them at all?

Well, magistrates' courts are the Wimpy Bars of the legal world – they're quick, they're cheap, and there's usually one just round the corner.

But, like a fast food shop, magistrates' courts have a limited menu. Don't expect them to give you a £10,000 lump sum and an order transferring the matrimonial home into your name. They won't – indeed, they can't.

If you are not setting your sights very high then magistrates are for you. Alternatively – and this is probably the best reason for asking magistrates for maintenance – you might not have made up your mind finally to apply for a divorce. This means you can't get maintenance pending suit from a divorce court, while the magistrates' courts are ideal because they don't require you to ask for anything except money.

Law Enforcement

> *Paying alimony is like buying*
> *oats for a dead horse!*
>
> American proverb

It's far from unusual for a wife to find that winning an order for maintenance is one thing – actually getting her hands on the money is another!

A husband or ex-husband may simply ignore the court order or the binding agreement he signed voluntarily; he may change his address and job, making it hard to pursue him through the legal system; he may even emigrate. In the last analysis, a man can always avoid obeying a court order, though only by taking extreme steps to impoverish himself, risking imprisonment in the process, or by exiling himself from the United Kingdom to live in a country whose courts do not enforce British court orders.

The vanishing trick

The one thing common to virtually everyone in the UK is a national insurance number, and it is through the national insurance system that vanishing husbands can be traced. If a man is in arrears with maintenance, his wife or ex-wife can fill in a simple form at the court, giving details of his last known address and place of employment. The court passes this information to the Department of Health and Social Security, who use it to trace his current job and home address. The new details are then given by DHSS to the court to help in enforcement proceedings – though they are *not* supplied to the wife.

Enforcing a voluntary agreement

If a husband and wife have reached a private, legally binding agreement about maintenance, and the husband fails to pay up, the wife can sue him for debt in the county court in the same way that his garage could sue him if he failed to pay a car repair bill. The fact that maintenance is involved does not give the debt any special status, as it would if the maintenance were being paid (or not paid!) under a court order.

The Lord Chancellor's Department published two very useful free booklets – *Small Claims in the County Court*, and *Enforcing Money Judgments in the County Court*. You can get them both from your local county court – you'll find the address in your phone book. Even if you employ a solicitor, it's handy to know what he's talking about, and the booklets explain a lot about legal procedure and terminology.

If there's a court order
There is no magic way a court can force a man to pay up if he is determined not to obey, but there are lots of ways a wife owed maintenance can try to get it before giving up.

REGISTERING THE ORDER WITH THE LOCAL MAGISTRATES
If a wife anticipates problems, or even if she just wants to be cautious, she can ask for a county court or High Court order to be registered in the magistrates' court for the area where her husband or ex-husband is living. This means the maintenance is actually paid to the magistrates' court, and then passed on to the wife. The court keeps a record of what's been paid so a wife will never have any problems providing evidence if there are arrears – if the husband isn't paying, the court is the first to know.

Advantages of registering:

* enforcement is simpler, faster and cheaper than in the higher courts;

* magistrates' court officials will often do for you a lot of the paperwork involved in enforcement proceedings;

* if the maintenance is so low you are entitled to claim some Supplementary Benefit as well, you can sign over a registered court order to the Department of Health and Social Security – they will pay you full Supplementary Benefit and take over themselves the task of chasing the husband for the maintenance payments due.

What the magistrates can do
The best weapon in the magistrates' armoury is the attachment of earnings order. Once they've seen that payments really are in arrears, the magistrates can order the husband's employer to deduct the maintenance from his wages or salary and send it to the court for forwarding to the wife.

This doesn't always work though. You can't attach the earnings of someone who is unemployed – because he hasn't got any – and you can't attach the earnings of a man who is self-employed either, because if he's not obeying the original court order he won't take any notice of attachment proceedings either!

Another drawback is the 'protected earnings' rule. This says an attachment order must not leave the man with insufficient to live on, support any other dependants he has, and meet other financial demands such as previous fines, court orders for debt, etc. The upshot is that after protected earnings are taken into account the man may not have enough left to meet the new attachment of earnings order.

More stings in this tale

Registering an order with the magistrates' court is not a one-way street to cheap and easy enforcement. Couples who go to the magistrates' court rather than the High Court or the county court generally have less money, and this is reflected in the size of maintenance orders made by magistrates.

When you go to the magistrates with a complaint about maintenance arrears, they do not always automatically take your side. They have powers to deal with the matter in other ways:

* they can cancel some or all of the arrears permanently;

* they can even reduce the amount of maintenance payable – and from the husband's point of view, it may well be easier to convince a magistrate than a county court registrar that the original order was too high.

There can be another disadvantage too: delay. Even if the husband pays up on time, simply getting the money through the magistrates' court machinery will mean that the wife won't get the money when she expects it. A delay of a fortnight seems typical, so if a wife expects to get her maintenance on the last day of the month she should actually budget to live without it until the middle of the following month!

On the other hand . . .
If a wife can get the magistrates on her side, she'll find they do have a very big stick they can wave: the power to send an erring husband to prison. This is most use if the husband is self-employed (and his earnings can't, therefore, be attached), and the court must, of course, be convinced that he has the means to pay the maintenance but is wilfully refusing or neglecting to do so.

ENFORCING AN ORDER IN THE HIGHER COURTS
If a maintenance order is made in the county court or the High Court, and is *not* registered in any magistrates' court, you have to go back to the higher court if the payer is in arrears and you want the order enforcing.

Remember!
☞ It's only when you use the magistrates' court – or register an order there – that the court will know when a payer really is in arrears. Payments under an order of the High Court or a county court go direct to the recipient, so if there are arrears the recipient has to *prove* that maintenance has not been paid. This means keeping an absolutely accurate record of payments all the time.

The higher courts can make an attachment of earnings order, just like the magistrates, and they can also issue a **warrant of execution** (no, not capital punishment for ex-husbands) or a **judgment summons**.

* A warrant of execution
A wife who believes her husband has goods such as furniture and other household effects, or a car perhaps, can apply to the county court in the area in which the husband lives for a warrant of execution. This orders the bailiff to go to the defendant's home or any other premises he has, and seize belongings worth enough to cover the arrears of maintenance.

The goods seized are sold at auction – but often, seizure is not actually necessary; the husband will back down at the last moment and hand over sufficient cash to cover both arrears and legal costs rather than see his hi-fi and his Cortina go under the hammer. (Quite right too – auction prices for second-hand belongings are always less than the items are worth to the original owners.)

* ### The judgment summons: go to jail, move directly to jail . . .

This is a request to the county court or the High Court for a person in arrears with maintenance payments to be sent to jail. It involves a formal court hearing at which the wife, or her lawyer, must prove the husband has the means to pay but has refused to hand over the money.

It is particularly useful as a threat when the husband can't be got at through an attachment or earnings order – perhaps because he's self-employed, or simply filthy rich and living off investment income. However, a wife who succeeds in getting her husband jailed may receive a terrific amount of satisfaction but nothing else, because he still won't have paid up.

SCOTLAND

In Scotland the system is slightly different. A wife whose husband has ignored a court order for maintenance enlists the help of a Sheriff Officer, who will try to collect the money for her. An interesting power he has, which isn't available in England and Wales, is that he can have the husband's wages frozen completely.

Death of a maintenance payer
When the recipient of maintenance dies, the payments stop. When the payer dies, it may not be so simple.

SECURED MAINTENANCE

This is straightforward maintenance payments backed up by an order that the payer must set aside some of his capital – stocks and shares, for example – to produce the same amount of investment income as the maintenance payments themselves. When the husband dies, the wife goes on getting her maintenance from the investments for the rest of her life, or at least until she remarries.

Needless to say, not many husbands are so rich that they have savings big enough to generate sufficient interest and dividends to match their obligations to pay maintenance! This is definitely one for the very wealthy only.

'AND TO MY FORMER WIFE, NOT A BRASS FARTHING ... ! !' Is nothing sacred? Husbands – and for that matter anybody else – who believe their last will and testament really is the last word on the subject of how their worldly goods are divided should think again.

Wives, ex-wives and children who are ignored in the will of a man paying maintenance, or are left less than they feel is right, can ask the court virtually to re-write the will, granting them a bigger slice of the cake. However, husbands anticipating an attack of this sort on their estate – and objecting to it – can ask the court to rule in advance that no such claim will be granted (see Chapter 10, pp. 104–6, where this is discussed in more detail).

All Change!
Nothing is forever, and maintenance orders are no exception. Once you are on the legal treadmill it can be very hard to get off. Once-and-for-all payments such as those involving a large lump sum or a transfer of property are not subject to second thoughts years later, but an order for maintenance can be altered at the request of either spouse whenever there is a significant change in circumstances.

What counts as a change
Courts are not keen on former spouses who demand a

recount at the drop of a very small hat, but these changes certainly do warrant a return match:

* unemployment, retirement or any similar major financial change in the circumstances of either the payer or the recipient of maintenance;

* re-marriage or permanent cohabitation of the payer, particularly to someone with children the payer then supports;

* re-marriage of the recipient – this ends the payer's responsibility, except for payments to his children, and he can demand the return of any maintenance payments he made *after* the remarriage;

* serious ill-health on the part of either payer or recipient, particularly if it affects ability to work or involves medical expenses;

* cohabitation by the recipient of maintenance, if the relationship is stable enough for the third party to be expected to make a financial contribution;

* additional expense involved in supporting a child as the child grows up.

When ex-husbands re-marry
One of the most unsatisfactory aspects of the way courts decide on the level of maintenance is that if a former husband marries again, and his new wife works, it is quite possible he will be ordered to pay his ex-wife more than if he stayed single.

The explanation is that the court might feel the second wife can then pay some of the household expenses previously shouldered by the husband. That would make him better able to afford to pay more to his former wife.

But, however you dress it up, the effect is that the second wife is helping to pay the maintenance due to the first, and every time she gets a pay rise, or moves to a better job, some of her money may end up in the bank account of the first wife. This is not a recipe for a harmonious second marriage.

Not every court applies this iniquitous rule, but many do, and the fact that it can be such a lottery makes a bad situation worse. If in doubt, all you can do is *not* re-marry.

Backdating

An amendment to a maintenance order can be back-dated to the date the variation was applied for. In 1984 this gave rise to what might have been a marvellous way for thousands of wives to reduce their tax by redirecting their own maintenance payments to their children.

Mrs Angela Morley-Clarke was divorced in 1969, winning an order for maintenance to be paid *to* her *for* her son. This was treated as her income and the money was taxed because she had a job paying more than her tax allowances. In 1979 she had this order varied so the payments went direct to the boy, using up his own personal tax allowance, so the net amount left after tax was enormously increased. She then won a further variation, to the effect that the change in recipient – from her to her son – should be backdated all the way to 1969.

This would have involved the Inland Revenue in making a very large tax refund, because they had cor-rectly taxed *her* as the recipient of the maintenance but were now being told the income was the boy's. The Inland Revenue refused to accept that income could be redirected after the event. An appeal by Mrs Morley-Clarke to the Revenue Commissioners failed, then she won in the High Court, but finally the Revenue were victorious in the Court of Appeal.

The upshot is, you can't gain any backdated tax advantage by having a court order varied to redirect your maintenance to someone with spare tax reliefs – though you can still, of course, do so with an eye to future tax benefits.

You can also ask the court, when applying for an

order, to make it operate from the time *voluntary*
maintenance payments were first made. Despite their
wariness over Mrs Morley-Clarke, tax inspectors will
accept this aspect of backdating – but only on these
conditions:

* both payer and recipient of the maintenance must
  agree;

* the backdating will be effective for tax purposes only to
  the date the court order was applied for – so voluntary
  payments before the application stay voluntary;

* the legal proceedings to have the voluntary payments
  made binding must have been carried through without
  any unreasonable delay.

3

Debts and Debtors

In London the main divorce court is the Divorce Registry at the palace-like Royal Courts of Justice in the Strand. The building itself is famous. Just as well known, by name if not by sight, is the street that contains the back entrance to the courts: Carey Street, known for being the route debtors take to the court dealing with bankruptcy. Together they provide a neat illustration of the way divorce and debt often go hand-in-hand, or rather back-to-back.

Debts? What Debts?

Many wives and not a few husbands have lived for years in blissful ignorance of the debts run up by their errant spouse. But even if yours is the type who pays every bill as soon as it arrives, don't forget the items you don't really think of as debts – things like gas, electricity, and telephone bills, mortgage repayments, and the rates. If your partner walks out, you'll be left holding the bills.

Broadly speaking, anyone in debt should be completely open with the person or firm to whom they owe money. Most creditors will prefer to work out a private agreement, perhaps for smaller repayments over a longer period, rather than face the cost and nuisance of a court hearing.

Joint Responsibilities

We are all responsible for our own debts, but a husband can also be held responsible for his wife's debts sometimes. If she runs up a bill at the butcher's, the butcher can sue the husband – though the husband can defend himself by showing he gives his wife enough housekeeping money.

Bank and credit card accounts in joint names are a different matter. A bank can demand that either signatory to a joint account should clear an overdraft, even if it was the other signatory who caused the account to dip into the red. And with credit cards, what counts is who applied for the card in the first place: they are responsible for the debts of the second cardholder.

Utilities

Different debts call for different measures. Gas, electricity and telephone bills are often the easiest problems to overcome. If you are a deserted wife whose husband was formerly responsible for these bills, your first move should be to ask the local accounts office for each service to transfer them into your name.

Do this as soon as the parting of the ways takes place. You'll find the appropriate addresses on the last bills you received, or in the telephone directory.

Don't linger in the hope that your ex will carry on forking out for services he's no longer using. He won't. Hanging on just means you'll run up debts. You may get the gas, electricity and telephone people to accept you as a new customer if you move fast, leaving them to chase your husband for payment up to the date you separated. But if you go to them three months after breaking up, they'll look to you for payment for those three months, and they may demand a lump-sum deposit as well, before switching the account to your name.

If you know there are arrears, don't let the situation slide – particularly where gas and electricity are concerned. Both industries have a code of practice setting down the rules covering disconnection, and helpful leaflets setting out these rules are available from show-rooms.

If you are faced with a sudden threat of disconnection, and there are children in the house, tell the gas and electricity accounts offices – and tell the local council's Social Services Department too. Social workers may be able to buy you a bit more time to pay.

Mortgages

Most mortgages are taken out by the husband; some are in joint names; very few are in the wife's sole name.

A wife left in possession of a matrimonial home on which mortgage payments are due should tell the building society or bank exactly what is happening, even if her husband has promised faithfully to keep up the payments. He might change his mind when he finds just how much it will cost him to house himself. If he does stop making the payments and the mortgage is in his name, proceedings for possession could be started against the husband – and the wife could find herself in deep trouble without knowing it until it's too late. There is an early warning system, though, and every wife in such circumstances should use it.

If she registers a charge on the property under the Matrimonial Homes Act – something dealt with in Chapter 6 (pp. 69–78) – this won't stop the building society bringing an action for possession, but it will mean they will tell her before going to court.

Building societies hate taking over homes and then selling them to recover their money. That's not what they're in business for. So keep the building society informed if you're having trouble getting your spouse to make payments. Tell the society if there's a court case pending. Don't just let the arrears mount up – that's a recipe for losing your home.

Rates

Rates are effectively a tax on the ownership and occupation of property. Even in today's climate of comparative sexual equality, most local authorities address rates demands to the husband, and it is the husband they will pursue through the courts for any arrears – at first, anyway – even though he is the partner likely to have left the matrimonial home.

If you don't pay your rates, the council will sue you, and, ultimately, use bailiffs to seize your property to cover the debt. Unfortunately for deserted wives, in practice this means the bailiffs would take furniture and other goods from the home in which the husband no longer lives – so the husband probably couldn't care less!

As with other debts, wives should let the council know as soon as possible after their marriage breaks up, particularly if the husband was paying rates by instalments. Ask for a few months' breathing space to sort out whether your husband will carry on paying voluntarily, or will have to be forced to pay maintenance to cover rates as well as other expenses.

Rent

If your home is privately rented, whether it's a flat or a house, responsibility for paying the rent rests with the tenant – the person whose name is on the rent book. It is that person the landlord will sue for possession of the property if the rent isn't paid.

What this means is that, if the husband is the tenant and he moves out and stops paying the rent, the wife could lose her home without having had any say in the matter, simply because it is the husband – and not she – who will be sued!

The wife's most important defence is the Matrimonial Homes Act, which gives her two very important legal rights:

* she can stay in the property right up to the date of the decree absolute as long as she takes over payment of the rent, even though she is not the legal tenant;

* she can apply for the tenancy to be transferred to her name, enabling her to stay in the property indefinitely.

From the Husband's Point of View . . .
Husbands should take a fairly calculating attitude to debts, preferably accepting their solicitor's advice on what they are likely to be forced to pay in the end.

- DON'T pay off debts one at a time.

- DON'T accept responsibility for specific expenses such as rent, HP payments, heating, etc.

- DO agree to make maintenance payments at a level high enough to cover all these expenses.

The reason for arranging money matters this way is quite simple. Husbands get tax relief on maintenance payments. They *don't* get tax relief when they send a cheque to the landlord, a cheque to the credit company, and a cheque to the gas board.

4

Legal Aid

There are two kinds of legal aid, plus a third option that isn't really legal aid but is extremely useful and cheap.

Thirty Minutes for £5
Although not part of the legal aid scheme, the Law Society's fixed-fee advice sessions are such good value they shouldn't be overlooked. The cost is £5, and that doesn't go up or down no matter how rich or poor you are. For this you get half an hour of a solicitor's time, allowing you to pick his brains to your heart's content.

Since time is money, sort out your questions in advance and take with you any documents you think he may need to see.

The fixed-fee scheme isn't operated by all solicitors so when you first contact a law firm make it clear you want a fixed-fee interview with a solicitor specialising in matrimonial law.

Legal Advice and Assistance
This is a halfway house to full legal aid. It is often called the **Green Form scheme** – logically enough, since this is the colour of the form you have to fill in to get the advice and assistance. The amount – if any – that you pay towards the solicitor's costs depends on your own income and capital.

(In Scotland, for some reason, the green forms are actually pink. So, if you live north of the border, for 'green' read 'pink' throughout this chapter!)

There is one big snag to the Green Form scheme. A solicitor can give you advice; he can give you assistance; but he can't appear in court for you except, perhaps, in the magistrates' court to deal with fringe matters like maintenance or custody. This means the solicitor *won't* be allowed to go to court and actually win a divorce for you under the scheme.

So what use is it?

Despite the more than slight drawback over court appearances (or, rather, non-appearances), the scheme has its advantages:

* The solicitor can tell you on the spot whether your financial position qualifies you for advice and assistance. (The full legal aid scheme can be very slow.)

* You get up to £50-worth of help, and when the £50 is used up the local legal aid office will usually agree to a request from the solicitor for permission to spend more.

Although you *can't* use the scheme to get a solicitor into court to win a divorce for you – or to defend one either – you *can* still make use of his knowledge. Under the Green Form scheme you can expect the solicitor to carry out a whole range of work:

* you can find out whether you have grounds for divorce;

* you can ask about the legal procedure for obtaining a divorce;

* the solicitor can write on your behalf to your spouse's solicitor to negotiate an out-of-court settlement;

* the solicitor can use the payment given him under the scheme to prepare an application for full-scale legal aid;

* the solicitor can act for you to register a charge on the matrimonial home so your spouse can't sell it without your knowledge;

* the solicitor can actually prepare your divorce petition – and if he does this, the £50 limit on costs is raised to £90.

Squeezing more out of the system
The Green Form rules say you can't split up your problems so you get £50-worth of assistance on divorce, another £50-worth on maintenance, a further £50-worth on an application for a property transfer, and so on. However, you can apply for a separate lot of advice on anything not strictly connected with your divorce or separation; debts, for example, come into this even though they may have arisen as a direct result of your marriage problems.

So, if you apply for help with your divorce, don't waste the time you're allowed by asking questions about things like bank overdrafts, HP arrears, or even your entitlement to supplementary benefit. Any of these problems can be put on a separate Green Form – winning you a further £50-worth of time.

Who can use the Green Form scheme?
Anyone whose income and savings – after certain deductions – are below a fixed limit can get legal advice and assistance under the Green Form scheme. You have to qualify on *both* counts – it's no use having a low income but big savings, or vice versa.

THE INCOME LIMITS
The qualifying income limits are changed from time to time, usually in November each year. The figures used below came into force on 25 November 1985.

What counts is your **disposable income** – the income you have left after paying certain expenses, such as supporting your family. *You can ignore your spouse's income if the legal help you need is because of some conflict* *with him or her.* Start with your weekly income before any deductions at all and then take off the following items:

£   tax and national insurance;

£   £34.50 if you are supporting your spouse;

£   £15.15 for each dependent child under 11;

£   £22.65 for each dependent child between 11 and 15;

£   £27.30 for each dependent child aged 16 or 17;

£   £35.40 for each dependent adult.

If what's left is less than £54, you get legal advice and assistance completely free of charge. If your disposable income is over £114 a week then you don't qualify – you have to pay your own costs. If your income falls between £54 and £114, what you pay is based on a sliding scale:

Weekly disposable income	What you pay
£54–62	£5
£62–67	£11
£67–71	£16
£71–75	£21
£75–79	£25
£79–83	£29
£83–87	£34
£87–91	£38
£91–95	£42
£95–99	£47
£99–104	£52
£104–108	£57
£108–114	£62

If you are getting Supplementary Benefit or Family Income Supplement you automatically pass the Green Form income test. That just leaves the examination of your savings to worry about.

COUNTING THE CAPITAL

To see whether your capital resources qualify for help under the scheme, add up all your savings, whether in cash, premium bonds, share certificates or similar investments. Include any valuable items you own such as jewellery or furs − but you can ignore other items of clothing. The value of your home can also be ignored, and so can your furniture − except for valuable antiques. The tools of your trade are left out of the calculation too.

Then make the following deductions:

£   £200 for your first dependant;

£   £120 for your second dependant;

£   £60 *each* for any further dependants.

If more than £3,000 (from March 1986) is left after making these deductions, you do not qualify for legal advice and assistance under the scheme.

The Full-blown Civil Legal Aid Scheme

Entitlement to civil legal aid is − like the Green Form scheme − based on your income and savings. But just to confuse you, all the limits are different, so even if you don't qualify for legal advice and assistance you may well be entitled to legal aid, which is better anyway.

The civil legal aid scheme covers the cost of a solicitor and, if you need one, a barrister as well. It can be entirely free, or you can be asked to make a contribution − it all depends on your own finances.

You *won't* get legal aid for an undefended divorce unless there's something peculiar about your case that makes it more complex than usual. Legal aid does cover the cost of all the paperwork and court appearances for:

*   a defended divorce action;

*   a contested case over custody of children, access, etc.;

*   maintenance applications;

* applications for lump-sum or property orders.

Broadening the scope

Strictly, legal aid is just that – aid of a legal nature. But if your spouse is self-employed, or a company director, or gets involved in complex business deals, your solicitor may not be the best person to check whether he or she is cooking the books to look poorer than is truly the case.

If you need a financial investigation of your spouse, get an accountant. But don't hire the accountant yourself – get your solicitor to do it. That way the solicitor foots the bill and there's a good chance it'll be covered, at least in part, by legal aid.

How to apply

The legal aid scheme could not be accused of going overboard to attract customers. For one thing, unlike the Green Form scheme where you get an on-the-spot decision, it takes about two months to get legal aid in a typical case and in a complex dispute the wait can be a lot longer.

There is a way of getting legal aid quickly in an emergency – for example, to get an injunction restraining a violent spouse – but you're very unlikely to qualify for this if all you are after is money.

If you are applying for legal aid remember one cardinal rule: YOU PAY FOR ANY WORK DONE BEFORE THE LEGAL AID CERTIFICATE IS GRANTED. The legal aid fund will NOT pay for work your solicitor does before the certificate is issued.

The best you can hope for is to qualify for a small amount of free, or cheap, work under the Green Form. In practical terms, this means work on your divorce grinds to a halt when you put in your legal aid application – and it doesn't get moving again until your solicitor gets his hands on that certificate. (Oddly, this does not apply in Scotland, where aid can be backdated to the time your application was received.)

The legal aid system is run by the Law Society, the solicitors' trade union, but the cash comes from the government, so it is actually DHSS officials who decide whether you meet the cash qualifications.

Your solicitor will give you the application form itself, but it is not a simple document. Among other things, it asks for details of your case, and a wrong answer could mean you'll fail to get legal aid. The solicitor will be happy to help with the form – but the snag is that if you ask for his aid he can charge for it. That's why it helps if you qualify for Green Form assistance, because you can use this to get the solicitor to fill in the form to apply for full legal aid!

Your application goes to the local legal aid office for them to pass judgement on the legal merits of your case. If they decide your case is hopeless, or frivolous, you don't get legal aid. The form also goes to the Department of Health and Social Security, who ask for masses of information about your income and savings. DHSS officials then decide whether your resources are small enough to let you qualify for legal aid at all, and how much, if anything, you will have to contribute to your legal costs.

The calculations are similar to those for the Green Form scheme. What counts is your disposable income – the amount left after certain deductions. You can ignore your spouse's finances because, in a divorce situation, you won't be able to draw on them anyway!

The income limits
The rules are revised from time to time – these came into operation on 25 November 1985.

Add up your expected *annual* income and then make the following deductions:

£   income tax and national insurance contributions;

£   job expenses, including travel costs and subscriptions to any trade union or similar association;

£   rent or mortgage repayments, and rates;

£   hire purchase payments;

£   insurance premiums;

£   any maintenance payments you are making to your spouse, if you are already separated;

£   £1,794 if you are still living with *and supporting* your spouse;

£   £788 for each dependent child under 11;

£   £1,178 for each dependent child between 11 and 15;

£   £1,420 for each dependent child aged 16 or 17;

£   £1,841 for each adult dependant.

If what's left after these deductions comes to no more than £2,255 annual disposable income, you'll get legal aid completely free.

If your disposable income is between £2,255 and £5,415, you will have to pay towards your legal costs. The *most* you will be asked to pay is a quarter of the amount of your disposable income between £2,255 and £5,415. For example: if your disposable income is £3,255, the first £2,255 is ignored and you can be asked to pay up to a quarter of the balance, £1,000, so your actual maximum payment would be £250.

On the other hand, if your disposable income comes to more than £5,415 a year, you don't qualify for legal aid at all.

The capital test
Remember that your savings *as well as your income* have to be below the legal aid limit. Add up all your savings,

including furs (but not other clothing), jewellery (but not your wedding ring or engagement ring), bank savings, premium bonds, shares and similar investments, and even the loanback value of life assurance policies.

You can ignore these assets:

£ your home, including the value of your furniture;

£ clothes;

£ tools needed for your job;

£ your car;

£ anything that is in dispute, such as property on which your spouse has a claim pending.

After leaving out the exempt items, if your disposable capital is less than £3,000 you pass the test completely – you'll get legal aid without making any contribution at all.

If your capital comes to between £3,000 and £4,710, you can be asked to contribute *everything you have* over £3,000 – in other words, you could be asked for as much as £1,710. And this is *on top of* any payment you have to make under the income test.

That can add up to a lot of money, but you should not be asked to put up more than the expected cost of your case, so you will not be made to hand over £1,000, for example, if your predicted legal costs are only around £500.

If your disposable capital comes to more than £4,710, you won't get legal aid at all, unless you are involved in an extremely unusual case in which the costs are expected to be massive.

There's no such thing as a free lunch
Or, as some folk say, you'll not get owt for nowt.

The sting in legal aid's tail is that if you win property or a lump sum of money as a result of a legally aided action, the legal aid fund will expect to cover its out-of-pocket costs from what you've won – unless, of course, they're paid by the other side in the case.

The first £2,500 of your winnings are untouched, and maintenance awards won't be attacked either, but lump sums of money or any sort of property are fair game for the legal aid fund.

This can obviously present problems involving your home. If you win a dispute over the matrimonial home, your victory will look a bit hollow if the legal aid fund then forces you to sell it to repay your legal aid.

In fact, what happens is that a charge is registered against the property. This means the debt to the fund is not actually collected until you sell the house. In the meantime, you've effectively got an interest-free loan.

What happens if you want to move house? This can be a problem. The Law Society will sometimes agree to what's called 'substitution' – transferring the charge to a new property, but they will apply a few tests first. You have to show that:

* repaying the legal aid fund when the first house is sold would cause you hardship;

* the new house will be worth enough to provide continued security for the amount due to the fund;

* the new property will be your only home and will also be a home for your child who is under 18 or still being educated, or the move is caused by your job, or for health reasons.

Re-marry in haste, repent in poverty?
If you can't wait to acquire a new spouse after winning a legally aided divorce, think twice. Marry within 12 months of getting your legal aid certificate and any wealth your new loved one brings with him (or her) might result in an increase in the amount of your contribution to the legal aid fund.

Legal Costs – How the Bill Climbs

> *One lawyer in town is poor;*
> *two lawyers in town are rich.*
> American proverb

In every divorce someone has to pay something. Even in a do-it-yourself case there are court fees. In a contested action there will almost certainly be two lots of solicitors' fees, two barristers' fees, plus VAT – and the court costs as well.

Law firms are just like any other business selling a service: some are cheap and some are expensive. In this context 'cheap' means around £35 an hour plus VAT, and 'expensive' really is expensive – £100 or more per hour, plus VAT. Both ends of the scale may seem a lot of money, but don't imagine you are putting £35 or whatever straight into someone's pocket. That fee covers the office rent and all the other administrative outgoings such as secretaries' wages, telephone and postal charges, etc.

If you go to a firm in a City of London skyscraper, where Sloane Ranger young ladies glide across deep-pile carpets to water the yucca trees, expect to pay for the ambience in the same way that you pay for the surroundings in a good hotel. If you want a lower bill – and that doesn't necessarily mean a lesser service – choose a firm with fewer frills.

How do you find out the cost before it's too late? Simple – you pick a few likely looking solicitors and ask their hourly charging rate. Don't be embarrassed – it's not an unusual question nowadays.

It's worth keeping an eye on your costs even if you expect the other side in your case to pick up the bill. If you are a wife hoping for lots of maintenance and a hefty lump-sum award, don't ring your solicitor every day with trivial domestic problems. Every time he picks up the telephone, the bill grows – and that will just make it harder for your husband to meet your demands at the end of the day.

Even if you win an order for costs when your case has been heard, don't count on that covering the whole of your solicitor's bill. You will get what the lawyers call 'party and party' costs, meaning you as one party to the case can recover your costs from the other party involved. But this only covers expenses you genuinely couldn't avoid in order to get justice. Any unnecessarily elaborate work is your responsibility, and what this means in a typical case is that you will get 80 per cent of your costs but you'll be stuck with 20 per cent of the bill yourself – unless your former spouse pays the lot voluntarily.

☞   A committee set up by the Lord Chancellor has recommended (August 1985) that it should not be possible in future for costs to be awarded against the respondent in an *undefended* divorce.

An interesting gamble

Husbands have open to them a method of possibly saving something in legal costs – but it's a gamble.

If a husband believes his wife will win a lump-sum order from the court, he can write to her before the case comes to hearing, making a firm offer. If the wife turns the offer down and the court then gives her *less* than the husband had offered, the wife may be ordered to pay the husband's costs from the date of the letter.

Of course, everything depends on predicting what the court will award the wife. You should not try this gamble (which is called a *Calderbank Letter*, after a case involving a couple of that name) without taking advice from a solicitor who at least has some experience of the level of recent awards, and therefore stands a chance of making a good forecast on your behalf.

How to Pick a Solicitor Who Knows What He's Doing

If re-marriage is the triumph of hope over experience, then getting divorced again is where the experience really pays off. About 20,000 people a year go through a second divorce, or even a third or fourth. They know what they are doing and they know how to make sure their solicitor knows what he's doing. Newcomers to the battlefield have to choose their own champion.

In theory, all solicitors know about matrimonial law because they have all passed the same examinations. In real life, though, it's not like this at all. Many solicitors specialise, so the lawyer you went to when you bought your house may be a whizz at conveyancing while barely knowing the difference between a decree nisi and a jam doughnut.

Personal recommendation is probably the best way to find a good solicitor, but if your friends are as inexperienced as you in getting divorced go to your local library or court. Ask to see the Law Society's list of solicitors in your area. This tells you which solicitors specialise in family law, and – very usefully – it also shows whether they take on legally aided clients or operate the £5-for-30-minutes scheme under which you can get basic advice face-to-face.

Another way to find a solicitor who knows the ropes is to contact the **Solicitors Family Law Association, Bouverie House, 154 Fleet Street, London EC4.** Members aim to avoid costly courtroom battles by negotiating agreed settlements.

A Cut-price Plan from the Barristers

Barristers have their own group specialising in matrimonial and similar problems – the Family Law Bar Association – and it runs its own voluntary conciliation scheme specially designed to settle financial disputes out of court at a fraction of the normal cost.

You still have to go to a solicitor in the first place. Legal protocol says members of the public can't go straight to a barrister – they have to be referred by a solicitor in the same way a GP puts patients in touch with a specialist.

But then, instead of preparing for a court case, the solicitor asks the FLBA to choose a barrister to act as referee. Both sides submit written details of their finances, and the barrister comes up with a settlement based on how he thinks a court would react if it were presented with the same information. You won't normally have to attend a meeting with the barrister, though if both sides want a face-to-face confrontation the FLBA may agree to it for an extra fee.

The big difference between this procedure and a full court case is the cost. In most cases, with maintenance to be settled but no big amounts of capital apart from the family home, the fee will be a flat £85. Even if large sums are involved, or there are family trusts or business accounts to study, the cost is likely to be no more than £150.

You don't have to be bound by the barrister's decision if you don't want to be, though both sides can agree to regard the decision as final if they wish. The same applies to the question of whether either side can go to court later and quote from the barrister's recommendation: unless both parties agree, you *can't* mention the FLBA decision in any subsequent court hearing.

You can get a free pamphlet about the voluntary conciliation scheme, and an application form, by writing to **The Clerk, Family Law Bar Association Conciliation Board, 2 Harcourt Buildings, Temple, London EC4Y 9DB.**

5

Breaking up – You and the Tax Man

A broken marriage doesn't just cause the obvious emotional, legal and cash problems. Less obvious difficulties are virtually certain to arise involving the tax man.

The first fact to grasp is that, to your tax inspector, divorce is not the important thing. **What matters to him is when you separated – because from then on you and your spouse are taxed as two single people.** It doesn't matter that you are still legally married – the tax man has his own definition of whether you are married or not!

If you are separated *in such circumstances as are likely to render the separation permanent*, then to the tax man you're single again. For this reason it is extremely helpful if you and your partner can at least agree on the date you separated, because you'll both be asked for this by your respective tax offices, and your answers will be checked against each other.

In cases involving a sudden walkout by one partner, the date of separation is clear. But what about on–off separations, or the partner who goes away for a holiday or business trip and doesn't come back? It's up to the two of you to decide when you actually stopped living together as man and wife, and with a fair degree of finality to the situation.

Income Tax

Whose income is which?
Unfair as it is, the law says a married man is responsible for paying the tax on his wife's income. It must be declared on his tax return, and he is the one who will be sued if the tax is not paid.

This burden vanishes on the day a couple split up, even if they stay legally married for the rest of their lives. On that day, the wife starts to be taxed as a single person again. The husband is still responsible for any tax due on her income up to the date of parting, but she pays her own tax after that.

Most working wives pay their tax under the Pay As You Earn system, so the practical effect of the change is barely noticeable. But high-earning couples will notice the difference. The husband does not have to pay the end-of-the-year higher rate tax demand on whatever his wife earns after they part; if her income after separation puts her in a tax band higher than the basic 29 per cent, the wife pays the extra herself.

What a relief . . .
After separation, the husband carries on getting the married man's tax allowance – £3,655 for 1986–87 – but only until the end of the tax year on the following 5 April. Then his allowance drops to the single man's rate, which for 1986–87 is £2,335.

He could carry on claiming the married man's relief right up to the date of the decree absolute as long as he was fully maintaining his wife by voluntary payments – but, as we've already seen, that would be very silly. From the husband's point of view, tax relief on maintenance payments made under a binding agreement is worth more than the difference between getting the single man's tax allowance and the relief given to married men.

For the wife's part, as soon as she and her husband split up she will qualify for the single person's £2,335 tax relief, even if she has already had the married woman's allowance of the same amount in the same tax year.

These personal tax allowances should present no problem because they are virtually automatic. Other reliefs may take some fighting for. If a couple have a joint mortgage but the partner who actually makes the payments leaves home and stops paying up, the partner who takes over responsibility for paying the building society, or the bank, should contact the Inland Revenue at once – otherwise, they'll get no mortgage tax relief, and the partner who isn't doing the paying any more will still reap the tax benefits.

Since the introduction of the MIRAS scheme, which gives tax relief on mortgage interest by cutting the amount of the monthly repayments, this last bit of advice does not apply to everyone. Mortgage interest relief at source (MIRAS) means the repayments and the tax relief go hand in hand. But not all mortgage lenders belong to the MIRAS scheme, and not all mortgages are included – some are left out because they are too big. To play safe, tell the tax office.

Child tax allowances – tax reliefs you claimed if you had a child under 18 or still in full-time education – were abolished some years ago, at the same time that Child Benefit, the weekly cash allowance, was made tax free. However, there is a special tax relief for single parents called Additional Personal Allowance (APA), explained in detail later in this chapter (pp. 62–5).

The Inland Revenue Department publishes a useful free pamphlet called *Income Tax – Separation and Divorce*. Copies are available from any tax inspector's office or PAYE enquiry office.

Tax Aspects of Paying and Receiving Maintenance
Whether you pay or receive maintenance you have to keep in mind the income tax consequences of what you are doing. If you pay maintenance you get tax relief on

what you pay, though just to confuse you there are various ways the relief can actually reach your pocket. In exactly the same way, if you receive maintenance there could be tax due on it, and there are various ways the tax might be collected.

There are two kinds of maintenance payments: payments from which tax has first been deducted, and 'small' maintenance payments, which the payer hands over in full.

The basic system

The normal rule is that payments of maintenance are made net of tax at the basic rate, which is currently 29 per cent. So, if a husband is ordered to pay his wife £3,000, he actually hands over to her only £2,130. He keeps back the other £870 – i.e. £3,000 @ 29 per cent. That is his tax relief, and as long as he actually pays £870 in tax on some of his income the tax inspector will not demand any of the £870 he's stopped from his wife's maintenance.

As well as the £2,130, the husband gives to the wife a piece of paper called a form R185, which he gets from his own tax inspector, or from the public enquiry counter at any handy tax office. Translating the jargon, this form says: *'I should have given you £3,000 which you are entitled to under a court order but I've deducted basic rate tax amounting to £870, so here's £2,130 instead.'*

If the wife has so much income, whether from maintenance or anything else, that she is liable to tax at 29 per cent, this is the end of the story. She was entitled to £3,000, tax has been deducted from it (just as though she had received £3,000 in earnings), and she is left with £2,130 to spend.

On the other hand, if the wife doesn't have enough income to make her pay tax – or not £870 of it anyway – then she can ask her own tax office for a repayment claim form. She fills this in to show her total income and then sends it to the tax office together with the R185 certificate showing she's already paid £870 in tax. If her tax bill should be less than £870, she gets a refund cheque.

Working wives can get a claim form from the tax office that deals with their employer's Pay As You Earn matters. Self-employed and non-working wives can get one from the tax office that deals with their home address – usually the one physically nearest you.

EXAMPLES

Suppose a man earning £10,000 a year is ordered to pay £3,000 a year to his ex-wife, who has no other income at all. This is how their respective tax positions will look, using 1986–87 tax allowances:

Husband		£
earnings		10,000
less single person's allowance		2,335
taxable income	=	7,665
tax at 29% on £7,665	=	2,222
		5,443
plus single person's allowance		2,335
income *after* tax but *before* paying maintenance	=	7,778
husband then pays to ex-wife £3,000 *less* tax at 29%	=	2,130
husband's net income *after* tax and maintenance	=	5,648

Wife		£
receives net maintenance payments		2,130
plus an R185 certificate showing tax deducted at source was		870
gross income	=	3,000
less single person's allowance		2,335
taxable income	=	665
tax at 29% on £665	=	192
		473
plus single person's allowance		2,335
wife's net income	=	2,808

This is made up of:

maintenance received from husband	£2,130
plus a refund of part of the £870 the husband deducted	678
	£2,808

IF YOU MAKE A MESS OF THE ARITHMETIC . . .

There are always some husbands who get the arithmetic wrong and deduct an incorrect amount of tax from the maintenance they pay to their former wife. Some simply don't deduct any tax at all, either because they do not know they should, or because the ex-wife has pleaded to be paid in full to help her cash-flow position.. ·,

Strictly, the deduction of tax from the payments is the husband's way of getting his tax relief. If he throws that away then that's his problem! However, while this is the law, the Inland Revenue operates a concession aimed at sorting things out where the ex-wife would be entitled to a refund of some or all of the tax that should have been withheld. In such cases, the payer does get his tax relief even though he failed to get it the right way, by deducting tax before paying the maintenance.

This is just a concession though. It is not a law, so it is not something you should rely on or demand as a right.

Small maintenance payments

Tax office staff would be buried under a mountain of paper if all ex-husbands deducted tax from maintenance payments and all ex-wives tried to reclaim it. So, when comparatively small sums are involved the payer hands over the lot and the recipient becomes responsible for paying any tax due on it.

The payer gets tax relief by having a higher than usual Pay As You Earn code number. Anyone paying £1,000, for example, will have their code increased by 100 points. That means they'll be allowed to earn an extra £1,000 before paying any tax. Self-employed people aren't covered by PAYE, of course. They have to wait for their accounts to be agreed after the end of the financial year, and then tax relief is given by an adjustment to their annual tax assessment.

The receiver of the money has to declare it for tax, though whether any tax is actually due depends on their personal circumstances – how much income they have altogether, and what tax reliefs they can claim. For the wife, the big advantage with small maintenance payments is that she gets all her money at once – she doesn't have to wait months for a tax refund to arrive.

WHAT COUNTS AS 'SMALL'
A small maintenance payment – one that has to be handed over in full – must meet two conditions: it has to be made under a court order – a private agreement won't do; and it must come within Inland Revenue limits, which are updated from time to time. For 1986–87 the ceilings for different types of payments are:

£   up to £48 a week *or* £208 a month if the payments are to a wife or former wife for her own maintenance;

£   up to £48 a week *or* £208 a month if the payments are made *to* someone under 21;

£   up to £25 a week *or* £108 a month if the payments are made for the benefit of someone under 21 – but are paid to someone else (a mother, for instance).

Payments above these limits *must* be made after deduction of tax at the basic rate.

Avoid the third option if you can. For the over-whelming majority of divorced or separated couples, making maintenance payments payable to the mother instead of to the children, who have their own tax allowances, is silly. You might just as well run up to the tax office door and throw your money inside because – in effect – that's what you're doing anyway!

EXAMPLES

Suppose a husband earning £12,000 a year was ordered to pay £150 a month (£1,800 a year) to his former wife, and that she also had earnings of £3,000. This is how they would stand with the tax man for 1986–87:

Husband		£
earnings		12,000
less single person's allowance	£2,335	
and maintenance paid in full	1,800	
		4,135
taxable income	=	7,865
tax at 29% on £7,865	=	2,280
		5,585
plus single person's allowance		2,335
husband's net income *after* tax and maintenance		7,920

Wife		£
earnings		3,000
plus maintenance received in full		1,800
		4,800
less single person's allowance		2,335
taxable income	=	2,465
tax at 29% on £2,465		714
		1,751
plus single person's allowance		2,335
wife's net income	=	4,086

The wife's tax, then, is £714 a year. But *all* this will be deducted under Pay As You Earn from her earnings of £3,000, because the money from the husband is paid in full under the small maintenance rules.

That means her weekly gross pay of £57.69 will seem to be very heavily taxed indeed, with about £13.73 a week going to the Revenue. Wives in this position have to convince themselves that it is still worth working, and that almost exactly £10 a week of those deductions refer to tax due on the maintenance, and less than £4 is tax on the wages.

'A verbal contract isn't worth the paper it's written on!'
With a few exceptions, which are not relevant here, contracts and agreements do not have to be in writing to be legally binding. A verbal contract can be just as effective. The snag is that the Inland Revenue won't accept a verbal agreement to pay maintenance *unless you put it in writing!*

You can turn this to your advantage though. If a couple simply split up, with the husband saying casually to his wife, 'Don't worry about money. I promise to pay you £100 a week until things are sorted out properly,' then that can be interpreted as a binding contract, with the wife able to sue for her £100 if it doesn't turn up.

The husband hands over £71, the other £29 being his tax relief, and the wife can reclaim part – or even all – of it, the amount depending on her own income and tax allowances.

Of course, it's very naughty for a couple to try to turn back the clock and convert an informal arrangement into something more concrete. For example, if no promises were made but a husband simply gave his wife £30 a week, the tax inspector would not be interested. The husband would get no tax relief on the payments and the wife would have no chance of getting a tax refund.

But if they later told the tax man there *was* a binding verbal agreement, that would mean the £30 wasn't really £30 – it was £42.25 from which the husband had stopped tax at 29 per cent. And the wife, if she had little or no other taxable income, would get back some or even all of the missing £12.25.

Needless to say, the tax inspector takes a dim view of couples who suddenly decide an informal agreement was really binding all along, and both parties would have to sign a declaration confirming the deal was meant to be legally binding.

You knew children were useful for something . . .
When the maintenance sums are being done children turn into little bars of gold – every one is worth as much as £677.15 in hard cash.

This is because children have their own tax allowances right from the moment they first draw breath. Just like single adults, they can earn up to £2,335 (1986–87 tax allowance) a year without paying a penny in income tax. Or, and this is the really useful bit, they can receive £2,335 a year in maintenance payments under a court order, all free of tax and without affecting their mother's tax position in the slightest.

EXAMPLE
Take a mother with £5,000 a year maintenance and one child:

		£
gross income		5,000
less single person's allowance	£2,335	
single parent's allowance	1,320	
		3,655
taxable income	=	1,345
tax @ 29% on £1,345	=	390
		955
plus allowances		3,655
wife's net income	=	£4,610

That means the wife doesn't have all the £5,000 to live on. She loses £390 to the tax man so her net spendable income is only £4,610.

But suppose the £5,000 which the husband pays is then split, with £3,000 going to the wife and £2,000 to the child. The result is:

		£
wife's gross income		3,000
less her tax allowances		3,655
taxable income	=	NIL
child's gross income		2,000
less child's tax allowances		2,335
taxable income	=	NIL

In other words, the mother keeps all of her £3,000 because as a single parent she can have up to £3,655 a year tax free. And the child keeps all of its £2,000 because it can have up to £2,335 tax free.

So, just by getting the court order phrased so that some of the available cash is paid to the child, the wife and child together have an extra £390 a year to spend – a saving of £7.50 a week.

From the father's point of view, he's still paying the same £5,000, so it might look as though he's getting nothing out of this scheme. But look at it this way: if the court order was solely in favour of the mother, and didn't direct some money to the child, it would cost him a lot more to have her end up with the same £5,000. For her to get £5,000 in her own name, the gross payments from the husband would, in fact, have to be £5,551 a year.

Not many people know this: one top firm of accountants reckons the tax man makes £125 million a year out of parents who don't sort out their maintenance arrangements properly, so letting their children's tax allowances go to waste.

GOING THROUGH THE HOOPS

There are two legal hoops you have to go through to make all this work:

* the payments from the father to his child have to be made under a court order – voluntary payments or even payments under an out-of-court separation agreement won't do;

* the court order MUST say that payments will be made TO the child – payments to the mother or to anyone else FOR the child won't work because the income won't be regarded as the child's by the tax man.

If a father does make payments to his child under 18 through a separation agreement, the tax inspector will ignore them. They will be treated virtually as pocket money for the child. The father will not get any tax relief, and he will have to make the payments out of his income, which has already been taxed.

And if the court order is worded so that payments are made to the mother, that's as far as the inspector will look. He will treat the income as belonging to the mother, even if the order goes on to say that the money should be used for the benefit and maintenance of the child.

IN SCOTLAND

Scottish law is slightly different, though you get to the same destination in the end. You cannot ask for an order making payments *to* a child, but the mother (assuming it is the mother who has custody) can ask for an order using what's called the **Huggins Formula.**

This is simply a form of words inserted into the court order to say that payments should be made to the mother as *curator* (trustee) for the child. In effect, this means that although the money is paid to the mother it is not legally hers to do with as she wishes – she is only receiving it on behalf of the child.

CONVINCING HMIT

As well as ensuring the court order is worded properly,

you may have to prove to the tax inspector that its terms are being carried out. It helps enormously to open a bank account in the name of the child and to pay the child's own maintenance into that. Of course, the mother can arrange the account to let her make withdrawals and sign cheques, so while the money belongs to the child it's not actually under his or her control.

Getting Tax Relief on School Fees

Any parent with a child going through the prep school or public school system knows that you don't get income tax relief on school fees. Divorce or separation changes all that! By using the child's own tax allowances, a father can actually arrange matters so that he pays the school in the normal way – but gets tax relief on the payments.

There are three ways of organising this, though one is far and away the best.

Paying the wife, who pays the school

The first option is for the father to make court order payments, or payments under a private agreement, to the mother. She then pays the child's school fees out of this income. Father gets tax relief on the payments, but the whole lot is then taxed as the mother's income. This wastes the child's tax allowances. Overall, this arrangement is financially inefficient. Some mothers may like it though, because it means they pay the school and they get a bigger say in their child's education – she who pays the piper calls the tune.

Paying the child, who pays the school

This is far better from a cash point of view than directing the money to mother. It uses the child's tax allowances, saving several hundred pounds a year. In practice, the money goes into a bank account in the child's name, but the mother can draw on the account. She actually pays the school from this account so – if she wants it – she keeps her influence at the school while the father need pay out less cash for the same result because less of the maintenance disappears to the collector of taxes.

Paying the school direct

This is the tricky option but it has all the tax advantages of paying the child – and two other bonuses too. Some fathers fear that if they pay money to the mother, or into a bank account she controls, she may fritter the cash away on herself. Then, when the school demands payment, she will put intolerable moral pressure on the father to pick up the bill rather than see little Johnny or Jilly slung out of school. That means the father effectively pays the same expense twice over – once in the maintenance cheque and then again direct to the school. Paying the school in the first place gets round this.

The other bonus is that when school fees rise (and who ever heard of a reduction in fees?), the amount father pays under the court order is automatically increased to match the rise – and so his tax relief goes up automatically too. There is no need to go back to court to ask for the order to be varied upwards, as there would be in any other change in personal circumstances. This is achieved by using a special form of words in the court order so that it doesn't mention a specific amount, but simply orders the father to pay an amount equal to the fees. Then, if the fees go up, so does the maintenance. This curious arrangement, under which it becomes possible for a father to get tax relief at anything up to 60 per cent on what is, after all, a very personal choice of how he spends his money, relies on a system of very definite arrangements.

PUTTING THE WORDS IN THE RIGHT ORDER . . .

Or even, put this order into the right words! The words that are crucial to the scheme are those that allow the amount the father pays to change from time to time. The court must use the following words, or some very similar, to order the father to pay:

> 'an amount equivalent to such a sum as after deduction of income tax at the basic rate for the time being in force equals the school fees charged by the school the said child attends for each financial year.'

A VERY NECESSARY CONTRACT

There is one further problem, and that is that the father must NOT be legally responsible for paying the school fees. The theory is that the father pays maintenance to the child and the child CHOOSES to spend the money on a good education!

If the father has made a contract with the school then all he is doing in paying the fees is keeping to that agreement. The court order becomes irrelevant, and father loses his tax relief. So, if father has signed the contract with the school he must terminate it, and the school must make a new contract with the child.

Most contracts are not legally binding on children, but those under which they purchase 'necessaries' are binding. Law books are littered with court cases brought over just what is, or isn't, necessary in a child's life. Education is said to be necessary, so a child *can* enter into a contract to pay school fees.

What happens in practice is that the contract also appoints someone at the school – usually the bursar – to act as the child's agent. The father then pays the fees to the bursar, who receives them in his role as agent for the child and then – switching parts – pays himself the money and accepts it in his role as a school official.

This multi-faceted gem of a scheme is necessary to squeeze the maximum tax and administrative advantages out of the situation. But the more people involved, and the more bits of paper flying around, the more chance there is that someone will take a short-cut and the whole arrangement will collapse. For safety's sake, get your solicitor to organise it initially, or at least go over the rules with your tax inspector in advance.

APA – The Single Parent's Tax Relief

Tax allowances are not cash awards. They are the amount you are allowed to receive each year before having to pay income tax. For 1986–87 a single person has an allowance of £2,335 and the married man's allowance is £3,655.

But single parents – whether separated, divorced, widowed, or simply unmarried – can claim an extra allowance of £1,320 if they have a child living with them. This is called the Additional Personal Allowance (APA).

You only get one allowance of £1,320 whether you have one child or a dozen. APA is granted on the basis of one allowance per claimant – *not* one allowance for each child. The rules covering APA were drawn up many years ago, when the typical single parent was a widow and divorce was far from widespread. They are simple to the point of being so loosely worded that some separated couples can actually be better off than when they were together!

* the relief is given only to parents claiming the single person's tax allowance for themselves – you can't claim APA *and* the married man's allowance, which usually means you don't get APA in the year of separation. (There are rare exceptions involving husbands with an invalid wife, but they are not relevant here.)

* to claim APA you must have a child resident with you for the whole or part of the financial year (6 April to the following 5 April);

* the child has to be under 16 or still in full-time education.

If the child spends time with both parents, they both have a claim to the allowance, and they can divide it between themselves however they like. If the parents cannot agree on a fair division of the relief, their tax inspectors will impose one based on the length of time they believe the child spends with each parent. Any parent unhappy with this official Judgement of Solomon has the right to appeal to the neutral Commissioners of Inland Revenue.

The Commissioners are local worthies, similar to magistrates except that they deal only with tax appeals. All the hearings are in private, and they are pretty informal so you don't have to be nervous about representing yourself. Be sure of your ground though, because the Revenue representative (probably an inspector from your tax office) will know his subject – and he'll have read your tax file, so he'll have a fair idea of what you are going to say before you have said it.

The loophole . . .
You may think the rule about each claimant being entitled to just one allowance leaves little scope for manoeuvre, but suppose there are two or more children, each of them spending some time at the home of each parent. Then, if the parents claim for *a different named child* each, they can both get the full allowance.

Tax inspectors do resist this. Their list of known excuses for refusing a double allowance includes:

● 'your children only stay at weekends and during holidays – they have to live with you full-time to qualify' – *WRONG: the law says the child need live with the claimant for only part of the year;*

● 'to claim APA you must have won legal custody of the child' – *WRONG: neither the law nor the Revenue's own internal instruction books lay down any such condition;*

● 'APA is only given to the parent receiving Child Benefit' – *WRONG: there is no link whatsoever between DHSS regulations on Child Benefit and Revenue rules on APA.*

● 'Just one allowance is available between the two parents, even if each parent claims for a different child' – *WRONG: there is nothing in either the law or the Revenue's instructions to local tax inspectors that bars a claim from both parents if they claim for different children AND the residence condition is met.*

It is the residence qualification that causes most rejections of claims to APA. The law itself lays down no minimum amount of time the child has to live with the claimant – it merely says the child must reside with the claimant 'for the whole or part of the year'. Confidential instructions from the Inland Revenue head office to local tax districts say this means a child's residence is:

'his usual place of abode . . . where accommodation is permanently set aside for him . . . and where he keeps clothes and personal belongings.'

This definition has never been tested in the courts. No appeal against a refusal of APA has yet got that far. But any parent lodging a claim should be aware that this is the test currently applied.

Revenue bosses accept that the law is vaguely worded, and they know local inspectors are – to put it diplomatically – uneven in the way they treat claims. For these reasons, all inspectors have been told that if a member of the public appeals against a refusal of APA, the appeal must *not* be referred to the Revenue Commissioners straight away as is the normal practice. First, the claim is re-examined by an expert at the Revenue head office just in case the local inspector has slipped up.

☞ **The moral is:** *don't give up, and don't accept that the inspector necessarily knows the rules better than you.* Many claims are accepted in full – but only after months of correspondence.

'I'll Pay the Gas Bill; You Pay the Rates . . .'

Some couples, when they separate, agree that the husband will pay specific bills instead of a set amount of maintenance. If the wife has any income of her own, she may agree to take responsibility for other outgoings.

From the wife's point of view this may be acceptable. She is, in effect, getting a blank cheque because any rise in domestic expenses included in the deal will be met by the husband and not her. The only possible drawback is that if she ever wants to borrow money, buy goods on HP, or even apply for a mortgage, she might have problems because, on the face of it, she hasn't actually got any income – money that she might regard as hers in fact goes straight from her husband to the gas board, British Telecom, or whatever.

From the husband's angle the whole idea should be avoided. It makes as much sense as mixing a cocktail in a colander. He is not entitled to any tax relief on the payments, even if the agreement is sanctified by a court order. He can get tax relief only if he is providing his wife with some income which, if her personal circumstances allow, can in turn be taxed in her name. Paying bills for her does not provide her with an income.

Husbands should insist that the wife add up the bills she wants paying, and then make the total the sum payable under a court order or other binding agreement which will count for tax relief.

The only exception to all this is the payment of mortgage interest, for which the husband can claim tax relief in some cases. Even here, though, husbands shouldn't be quick to undertake payment. It could complicate their own mortgage tax relief if they are buying another property, and they can do much better by having the payments absorbed into a court order as a defined sum, giving them tax relief on the capital repayments as well as the interest.

Capital Gains Tax

How separating cuts the bill

Most people don't pay capital gains tax because they simply don't make capital gains. CGT is the tax charged on profits you make when you sell an investment at a higher price than you paid for it. You get relief for inflation since March 1982, and you are allowed a certain amount of gains tax free in each financial year – £6,300 for 1986–87.

Transfers of assets, such as shares or valuable antiques, between a husband and wife are ignored by the tax inspector. He does not charge tax on a disposal from husband to wife or vice versa, as he would on sales or gifts to other people. In practice, Revenue officials take this line right up to the end of the tax year in which a couple separate, so it is possible for a couple still on speaking terms to rearrange their investments without paying tax even though they are no longer living together as man and wife.

Gains made during the year of separation are split by

the tax man: the husband must pay any tax due on his own gains for the whole of the year. However, he's allowed to claim relief for any losses made by his wife before they parted.

It's not all plain sailing though. The husband has to pay any gains tax due on profits his wife made before they split up, even though he may not be able to get at the profits if they've been reinvested in his wife's name.

The wife becomes responsible for her own gains tax as soon as she and her husband part. She gets her own personal exemption of £6,300 (1986–87) to use in the remainder of the tax year in which separation takes place, and she gets relief for her own post-separation losses. Any losses she'd notched up before separation stay with her husband for him to use to cut his tax bill on any of his own future gains!

Special exemptions
There is no capital gains tax when only money is changing hands rather than actual assets. No tax is due on lump-sum *cash* awards arising from divorce or separation proceedings.

☞ **Remember!**
A husband whose savings are tied up in, say, shares should tell the court how much gains tax he will have to pay if he sells shares to enable him to pay a lump sum to his wife. The court will only look at the net proceeds of the sale in deciding how much he can afford.

There is a special gains tax concession involving the matrimonial home, allowing it to be transferred from the spouse who's left to the spouse who's stayed without any liability to gains tax, even as late as two years after separation. There are more details of this in Chapter 6 (pp. 76–7).

Gifts Tax
Capital transfer tax (the proper name for gifts tax) will cause no problems now as it was abolished on lifetime

gifts in the 1986 Budget. It was replaced by an inheritance tax, which applies primarily to bequests on death, though it can catch gifts made shortly before death as well. However, the rules that did apply to lifetime gifts are worth a brief mention for the sake of couples who have already parted.

Husbands and wives paid no CTT on any cash or assets passing between them during the lifetime of their marriage – and that meant right up to the date of the decree absolute. This exemption applied as long as both spouses were domiciled in the United Kingdom – which means, roughly speaking, that the UK was their permanent home country.

After the decree absolute took effect this exemption was lost. The couple became just like any other individuals, and major gifts (if they still felt like making them!) from one to the other did count for transfer tax – which meant you could give away £67,000 (1985–86 figure) in any 10-year period before paying CTT at rates that started at 15 per cent and rose to 30 per cent (rates for bequests as opposed to lifetime gifts were doubled). On top of the £67,000 allowance spread over 10 years you could also give away £3,000 a year in all, plus as many small gifts of up to £250 as you liked.

There were also two very useful exemptions just for couples who were parting. The first covered property transfers made under a court order. These *didn't* count as gifts so there was no gifts tax to worry about. The second exemption covered maintenance payments, whether under a court order or private agreement. These didn't count as taxable gifts as long as they were made by one spouse or former spouse to another, or to a child of either spouse.

In fact, Revenue officials only sat up and took a lot of notice when a father tried to use this last exemption to make big transfers of property or investments to his children. Dads trying this one may well have found it a mite difficult to convince the tax man that little Johnny or young Sarah really needed the title deeds to a farm in Sussex, or 500,000 shares in ICI, just to maintain a decent standard of living. He might have suspected the real motive was tax evasion!

6

Home Sweet Battleground

'The matrimonial home is usually the most important capital asset. Often the only one.' So said Lord Denning, perhaps Britain's best-known twentieth-century judge, in a trend-setting 1973 case in which he decided that a wife should have a share in the home when a couple split up, whether or not she had actually contributed money towards the purchase price or the mortgage repayments.

Whether a home is owner-occupied, paid for, mortgaged, or rented, who gets it – and on what terms – is likely to be the biggest source of conflict between husband and wife now that actually getting the divorce itself is comparatively easy.

Rented Property

In most cases the tenancy of a rented property will be in the name of the husband. If he moves out and ceases to pay the rent, the wife may find the owner of the property starts legal proceedings for possession of her home. If this happens, the action will be brought against the husband – because he's the tenant – but the wife can ask the court to name her as a defendant in the action too. If she does this, she stands a good chance of getting any possession order frozen as long as she takes over responsibility for paying off any rent arrears.

A wife is also entitled to stay put in rented property right up to the date of any decree absolute, and the landlord must accept rent from her – he can't refuse rent from her and then try to claim possession because the husband, the real tenant, is in arrears.

These are temporary points though. In the long term, if she wants to stay in the rented property, the wife has to have the tenancy transferred to her name. If *no* divorce is in the offing the wife can ask the court to make an order under the **Matrimonial Homes Act**, making the tenancy over to her – but both the husband and the owner of the property are entitled to turn up in court and object.

If a divorce is planned, a transfer of the tenancy can be requested as part of the same legal proceedings, killing two birds with one stone. And if the landlord is proving objectionable over a transfer of the tenancy, a wife can do herself some good by arranging things this way and deliberately making the tenancy transfer part of the divorce proceedings and not a separate action. This is because, curiously, although the landlord can object to a transfer when it is requested in a case on its own, he doesn't have the right to do so when the transfer is decided as part of divorce proceedings!

Scotland

In Scotland a wife's rights are built on a better legal foundation than in England and Wales. Under the unimaginatively entitled Matrimonial Homes (Family Protection) (Scotland) Act, 1981, a wife has the right to stay in the matrimonial home even if the husband is the legal tenant, and she cannot be thrown out.

So You Own Your Own Home

Well, forget any notion of it being your castle. Even if you own your home completely, with no outstanding mortgage, and you paid every penny of the purchase cost, a court can still do what it likes with your property. Usually, it does one of the following:

* transfers ownership from one spouse to the other;

* defines the share of the property owned by each spouse, but postpones a sale until some future date – when the children have finished their education, for example;

* orders an immediate sale, and says how the proceeds should be split up.

How the court makes up its mind

There are no hard and fast rules about how the courts decide who gets what in relation to the matrimonial home. It would be an exaggeration to say that judges make it up as they go along – but only just. Broadly speaking, these are the things that will influence the court, though no single factor is enough to guarantee victory:

* how long the marriage has lasted;

* the ages of the husband and wife;

* whether there are any children, and how old they are;

* the availability of alternative accommodation if one spouse (usually the husband) is deprived of the matrimonial home;

* who paid for the property and – if it is mortgaged – whether cash is available to continue the repayments.

If the marriage has not lasted long, and if there are no children, the court may simply try to unscramble the omelette and give both partners back whatever they put in. The simplest way to do this is to order that the home be sold and the proceeds divided in whatever way the court wishes. Either partner can, of course, buy out the other partner's share if he or she wants to stay in the property – and can afford to do so.

If the marriage has lasted some years, the court is less likely to place much importance on who paid what when the home was bought. In other words, the value of a wife's housework starts to have an influence. It is still quite probable that an immediate sale will be ordered, but the way the proceeds are split might bear little relation to the partners' original contributions. Typically, the wife who has made little or no cash contribution towards buying the property might be awarded a share of between one-third and a half.

In addition the court might decide not to order a sale at all for the moment. This makes sense if the proceeds would not be enough to enable both parties to find new homes – and even more sense if a sale would simply attract a claim from the legal aid fund for repayment of their costs.

Despite the fact that this is a pretty messy solution, the court can allow the wife to stay in residence for as long as it likes, possibly paying rent to her husband, or ex-husband, for the use of whatever share of the property the court awarded him.

If there are children, then the court's priorities are geared completely to their welfare. Typically, the court will order that the wife and children can stay in the matrimonial home until the children have finished their education. This assumes that the husband can afford to keep up any mortgage repayments, or that he will pay the wife enough maintenance to allow her to take them on!

If this is financially impossible, and the house has to be sold, the division of the proceeds is certain to be slanted towards allowing the spouse who gets custody of the children (virtually always the wife) the lion's share of the cash to go towards a new, cheaper home.

GETTING A SLICE OF THE ACTION

In any case involving a postponed sale, the husband should make sure his share of the house is expressed as a percentage and *not* as a fixed sum. A half share in a house currently worth £50,000 will, if it's expressed in cash, still be worth £25,000 in 15 years' time. But if the court grants him 50 per cent of the property he'll get half of whatever it fetches when it's eventually sold – and that should be an awful lot more than it's worth now.

All this is, of course, after a case has actually got to court – but the problems can start much earlier.

Stopping the roof over your head being sold behind your back

A house can be sold by whoever's name appears on the title deeds, irrespective of the rights of the other marriage partner. Intending wives might like to bear this in mind and ask that the matrimonial home be bought in joint names from the start!

If a wife is afraid her husband may sell their home as soon as the marriage starts to crumble (or even if she is merely prudent), she should register her right to stay in the property. This involves placing a note on the records of the Land Registry or the Land Charges Department – in short, it's the equivalent of waving a huge red flag in the face of anyone considering buying the property! A Scottish spouse whose name is not on the title deeds has the right to stay put anyway – the spouse who does legally own the home can't sell it behind the other's back.

GETTING THE PAPERWORK RIGHT

Most homes are now registered property, which means the title records are held by the Land Registry. Officials will supply you with forms to register your right to occupy the property and they'll also give you the necessary facts about the registered title number, etc, so you can fill in the details.

If your home is not registered, you should contact the Land Charges Department and ask to register a 'Class F' charge against the property.

- The Land Registry head office is at Lincoln's Inn Fields, London WC2.

- There are District Land Registries elsewhere – addresses are in the telephone directory.

- The Land Charges Department is at Burrington Way, Plymouth.

TWO TIPS

* If you don't know whether the title to your home is registered or unregistered, the quickest way to find out is probably to ask the bank or building society that supplied the mortgage.

* If you are entitled to legal aid or the more limited legal advice and assistance, this will cover the cost of registering your interest in the matrimonial home, so you can get your solicitor to do all the paperwork.

AND FINALLY . . .
Registration only lasts until the decree absolute. If you want to extend it – if you still haven't sorted out a divison of property – you have to ask the court for permission. This is, of course, less of a worry in Scotland, where spouses have automatic occupation rights.

Scotland
In Scotland, if you want a property transfer order you have to apply for it *before* your divorce is granted. You cannot apply afterwards.

Tax Problems
Property transfer orders can throw up all kinds of tax problems, probably the biggest of which involves mortgage tax relief.

Mortgage misery . . .

Tax relief is available only on the interest you pay on your mortgage, not on the capital repayments, and only on mortgages up to a certain limit – for the tax year 1986–87 the limit is £30,000. If you have a £50,000 mortgage, you only get tax relief on three-fifths of the interest. This can cause big problems if you have – for example – a £20,000 mortgage on your matrimonial home, and your marriage breaks down, leaving you looking for a further £20,000 loan to buy yourself a new property. The two mortgages would take you over the £30,000 ceiling.

. . . AND HOW TO BEAT IT

The way round this is for the husband to transfer both the house and the responsibility for the mortgage to his wife. She then makes the mortgage repayments out of money he supplies under a court order. The result is that tax relief is available on both mortgages, because both husband and wife – once separated – are allowed relief on a full £30,000 loan. And almost as a side effect, the husband also gets tax relief on the *capital* repayments on the original home, not under the rules for mortgage tax relief but because the payments are under a court order.

Making the wife responsible for the repayments may not be easy. The building society or bank might take some convincing that she can keep up the payments. But they will often be swayed if the husband stands guarantor, pledging to cover any default by the wife or ex-wife. Offering a guarantee like this won't affect his ability to claim what is, in effect, a double helping of tax relief – but it might well be the clinching factor in whether he gets it or not.

A word of caution!

☞ Part of the small print in the rules on who gets mortgage tax relief says that you only get relief if you are the owner, or joint owner, of the property in question. So, if a husband transfers the matrimonial home to his wife but carries on making the mortgage repayments, he'll have signed away his tax relief along with his home.

You can get round this by keeping an interest in the property, but this still leaves you subject to the £30,000 ceiling. All in all, there's a lot to be said for transferring the property to the wife and consolidating the mortgage repayments into the maintenance.

How gains tax can take a slice of your divorce settlement
Why should gains tax cause any problems for couples whose marriages break down? Well, the tax inspector doesn't just concern himself with investment sales that actually create a real profit. To him, any disposal of an asset counts – even a gift – as long as the item changing hands is worth more than when it was originally acquired.

Just consider the matrimonial home. The basic rule is that a man's (or woman's) home is his (or her) tax-exempt castle. Profits on the sale of your main residence are *not* taxed. But we are all allowed just one castle each, and we have to live in it.

The result should be that if a husband leaves home he loses the gains tax exemption on that house. However, Revenue officials have spotted this point, which seems to have been overlooked by Parliament, and they've devised their own rule to get husbands off the hook.

This says that a husband can move out of the matrimonial home and later transfer it into his wife's name as part of a financial settlement, and still escape gains tax – even though the property may not in fact have been his home for up to two years.

There is a snag though: to hang on to the exemption on his old home, the husband can't have a new property that is also gains tax free. If he's in rented property this is no problem – but if he's buying a new house or flat for himself and it's rising in value, he's clocking up an eventual liability to CGT.

There is an answer, of course! If there is another woman on the scene, the husband can put the new property into her name, since she comes complete with her own gains tax exemption on what is, in the tax man's eyes, her own home. As soon as the financial loose ends from the first marriage are all tied up, the ex-husband can safely marry his new property-owning lady and keep the gains tax exemption intact.

EVERY SILVER LINING HAS A CLOUD . . .

In this case, it's a court order allowing one spouse (usually the wife) to stay in the home, perhaps until the children have grown up years later. The husband keeps his stake in the property – whatever the court awards him – but the house is not actually sold so he doesn't get his hands on his share of the money for a very long time.

When the property is eventually sold, the spouse who stayed in the house has no gains tax worries. It was her main residence, probably her only one in fact, so her gain is exempt from CGT.

No such luck for the husband. He may have been part-owner of the property, he may not have owned another home since the divorce or separation – he could even have been sleeping on the Embankment for 20 years! The tax laws are blind to such things: because he was not living in the house it is, in tax law, an investment intended to show a profit – and a taxable profit at that. If the husband's share of the proceeds of sale is big enough (i.e. it exceeds that year's CGT threshold), he pays gains tax at 30 per cent.

Rather than have funds locked up for years in a property that can't be sold, and that will eventually be taxed anyway, some husbands give up their claim to any slice of the home in return for paying a lower lump sum, or a smaller amount of maintenance. The arithmetic has to be individual in every case but this is probably a good example of making the best of a bad situation.

Stamp duty – the old tax that refuses to go away

Stamp duty is the oldest tax in the Inland Revenue's present-day bag of tricks. It dates back to 1694, and despite numerous calls for its abolition it is still here because governments and civil servants love it. They love it because it is terribly easy to operate – other people do almost all the work – yet at the same time it brings in large amounts of money, over £1 billion a year.

Stamp duty is a tax on certain legal documents, including those transferring property from one person to another. If the property is worth over £30,000 (the threshold for 1986–87), then duty is due at 1 per cent on the whole of its value, *not* just the bit over £30,000.

The good news is that since the 1985 Budget if a court orders property, such as the matrimonial home, to be transferred from one spouse to the other as part of proceedings for divorce or judicial separation then the normal stamp duty levy is replaced with a merely nominal demand for 50p.

The bad news is that officials in the Stamp Duty Office sometimes look behind the bare details of the property transfer and try to show that the horse-trading that's gone on amounts to a sale by one spouse to the other of his or her interest in the home. Then, full stamp duty is due.

Couples discussing the future of a matrimonial home in which the stake under negotiation is worth over £30,000 should make sure their solicitor words the proposed court order carefully to avoid any suggestion of a deal on which a cash value can be placed!

Enforcing the Order You've Won

As with maintenance, winning a court order is one thing but you may have to enforce it.

If a husband refuses to sign the necessary documents transferring the matrimonial home to his wife, or into joint names or the names of trustees, then the court will simply do it for him and run up his legal costs at the same time. There is no point in refusing to sign except, perhaps, nuisance value if that's what you want.

7

'And on Top of the Periodical Payments, a Lump Sum . . .'

As well as being able to order one spouse to make periodical payments (maintenance) to the other, or to children, the court can decide that a lump-sum payment should be made – either instead of regular maintenance or on top of it. The aim is to divide savings fairly, in the same way that the matrimonial home is considered as an asset to be shared. Unlike maintenance, though, you only get one bite at the cherry. A lump sum is meant to last forever, and if a wife is awarded £5,000 this week only to see her husband win the pools next week, well that's tough luck on her!

Odd spot
Magistrates' courts seem to have escaped the rule against asking for more. Although magistrates' powers are very limited – they can't divorce people, for example – they can order a lump-sum payment of up to £500, and it appears there is no limit to the number of times they can do this as long as they stay within that ceiling each time!

What the Wife Should Do

A wife who wants to apply for a lump-sum award should go to court armed with two bits of knowledge:

* the value of the couple's savings, investments, businesses, and other capital assets;

* the expenses she had to meet *after* the marriage broke down but *before* she began to receive maintenance, and that should normally have been the responsibility of her husband.

Remember!

☞ It's not all one-sided. Any savings the wife has in her own name are taken into account in deciding who gets what.

What the Husband Should Do

Lump-sum awards could become very popular in future as the 'clean break' idea of divorce takes hold. You can't have a clean break when one party has to send the other a cheque every month and there are recurring battles every few years for a rise – or a cut – in maintenance. A lump sum is a once-and-for-all payment leaving you poorer but able to re-start your life without strings.

Husbands favouring a lump-sum deal should bear in mind two things:

* If their savings are tied up in shares or similar investments, they could face a hefty gains tax bill when they sell up to raise money for a lump-sum settlement; the court *will* take this into account – it's only the *net* amount available after tax that counts, so talk to your broker and do your sums before going to court.

* Try to find out whether your wife has a new husband lined up; there's no point in handing over a hefty lump sum to get out of paying maintenance for life if you'd be let off the hook in a few months anyway because your ex had remarried!

Anything You Sell May Be Used in Evidence against You

Two words of warning.

☞ If you think you are about to be hit with a lump-sum order, don't go out and flog the family silver or immediately go on a wild spending spree – or transfer all your shares to your lover. It won't work.

The court can look back at all such disposals of assets in the three *years* up to the date the lump sum was applied for, and unless you can produce evidence to the contrary the court will simply behave as though you were deliberately getting rid of your savings and not engaging in a legitimate and justifiable deal.

☞ *Both* sides have a legal duty to put all the relevant facts before the court. This means a wife should not conceal any wedding plans she has just so she can get a lump sum now.

One particularly stupid wife recently couldn't resist flashing her new engagement ring at her husband as they entered court, whereupon she slipped the ring into a pocket – only to be ordered by the judge (tipped off by the husband) to produce the ring again so he could have a look too! Needless to say, the lady left the court with a very red face and no lump sum.

In another case, five Law Lords unanimously allowed an ex-husband's appeal against a *consent* order under which he agreed to give his former wife his £12,000 half-share of the matrimonial home in Cornwall. He had agreed to give up his share of the house in return for the wife not claiming maintenance – but two days later she remarried, so any maintenance payments would have ceased then anyway! Because she failed to disclose her marriage plans, the Law Lords allowed the husband to call the deal off.

Lump Sums and Tax

Lump-sum awards are normally free from *gains tax* in much the same way as property transfer orders.

For *income tax* purposes, however, there can be a problem – or at least one more thing to take into account. Lump sums don't count for income tax – the payer doesn't get tax relief, and the recipient isn't taxed. So, if a husband is planning to pay a one-off lump sum in return for saying goodbye to regular maintenance payments he should take into account in his calculations that he's also kissing his tax relief goodbye. What he should compare is the size of the proposed lump sum against the *net* cost of making maintenance payments, after he's had his tax relief.

Enforcement

If a husband ignores an order to pay over a lump sum of cash, the court can just order a sale of his property or investments, depriving him of the choice of what's sold and also taking away his option to borrow the cash if he doesn't want to sell assets.

Scotland

A subtle but important difference between the law in England and Wales and the law in Scotland is that, in Scotland, once you have got your divorce it is too late to apply for a lump sum. You have to ask before the divorce is granted.

8

Benefits and Pensions

Anyone who believes two can live as cheaply as one has
never been involved in a divorce. Not every marriage
breakdown involves a lump-sum settlement, a transfer
of the matrimonial home and a promise of periodical
payments every month for decades to come. Many
break-ups leave one – or both – partners with insufficient money to live on, possibly struggling to maintain
themselves and their children on state benefits.

A time when you are in an emotional turmoil is
certainly not the best moment to pick for a crash course
in the often messy social security system; but the blunt
fact is that you have little choice but to learn quickly if
you are to survive financially. To a large extent the
system means you have to know what to ask for and
what you're entitled to – the meek shall inherit very
little, unfortunately.

The government is currently undertaking a massive
review of the social security laws, with big changes due
to come into force in 1988. On top of this, the amounts
paid under the various benefits normally change each
year. New benefit rates used to be introduced every
November, but it is planned to alter this to April, in line
with the start of the new income tax year.

If you have any doubts at all about qualifying for a
benefit, or the amount due, the golden rule is to *ask*.

You can get advice from your solicitor – though it has to be said that many lawyers display a knowledge of state benefits just about on a par with their knowledge of dragon-slaying, alchemy and pseud-epigrapha.

Citizens' Advice Bureaux and law centres are often a better bet, or you can simply pick up a telephone, dial 100 and ask for **Freefone DHSS.** That will put you through, at no charge, to a DHSS enquiry unit whose officials will give advice in principle on anything to do with state benefits or national insurance.

State benefits fall into two classes: those that everyone can claim, whatever their income, and those that are means-tested. All are *cash* allowances – unlike income tax allowances, which merely represent the amount of your own income you can keep free of tax.

The benefits most likely to be of help if you are divorced or separated are:

- Child Benefit

- One Parent Benefit

- Child's Special Allowance

- Family Income Supplement

- Supplementary Benefit

- Housing Benefit.

Child Benefit
This is currently £7.10 a week for each child (from July 1986). It is tax free and you can claim it even if you have made no national insurance contributions at all, and whatever your income. You must be responsible for a child who is under 16, or under 19 and still in full-time education.

The child need not be living with you, but if it is not

then you must be contributing to the child's maintenance at a rate at least equal to the amount of Child Benefit you want to claim. Either parent can claim, but in a separation or divorce priority is given to the parent with whom the child actually lives.

One Parent Benefit

This is a top-up of £4.60 a week (from July 1986), added to your Child Benefit. It is a flat-rate sum – you don't get more for having more than one child. It is tax free, not means-tested and not linked to past payment of national insurance contributions.

To get it, you have to be separated or divorced and bringing up a child single-handed. You qualify after living apart from your spouse for 13 weeks or – if you can arrange it sooner – by being divorced or judicially separated. You lose the benefit if you start living with someone (including your former spouse) in a man–wife relationship.

Child's Special Allowance

This is £8.05 a week for each child (from November 1985 – it was not increased with other benefits in July 1986). It is paid to a divorced mother whose maintenance has ceased because her ex-husband has died. The allowance is tax free, but it *replaces* the One Parent Benefit – you can't have both.

There is no means test, but you have to meet the rules for claiming Child Benefit *and* your ex-husband must have paid a certain number of national insurance contributions at some stage in his life. The allowance has to be claimed within three months of the ex-husband's death, and you lose it if you re-marry or live with a man in a man–wife relationship.

The national insurance conditions are that the ex-husband must have actually paid 50 flat-rate contributions (of any class) at any time before 6 April 1975, *or* he must have actually paid contributions on earnings of at least 50 times the weekly lower earnings limit in any one income tax year.

The lower earnings limit is the level of income below which no NI contribution is charged. It normally changes every year, so in practice, unless you know your ex-husband's earnings were such that he was certain to have been paying national insurance contributions, the simplest – and probably the only – way to find out whether he paid in enough to allow you to claim Child's Special Allowance is to ask the DHSS to check for you.

Family Income Supplement

This is a cash payment for people on low earnings who have at least one child under 16, or under 19 but still in full-time education. It *is* means-tested – the amount you get depends on how much you earn and how much other income, such as savings interest, you have, as well as on the size of your family. FIS is meant to help people in work, which means that to get it you have to work at least 24 hours a week if you are a single parent with a child at home.

Getting the benefit does not depend on how many national insurance contributions you've made. FIS is tax free and, once you've got it, it won't be taken away, or reduced, for a year – even if your income goes up during that time. Remember this when timing an application for more maintenance – it's better to get a rise in maintenance just *after* a rise in FIS, not just before.

To get FIS the family's weekly income (ignoring a small number of items, the only important ones being Child Benefit and rent allowances or rebates) has to fall below these limits (set in July 1986):

	Weekly income
family where child is:	
under 11	£98.60
11–15	£99.60
16 and over	£100.60
increase for each additional child:	
under 11	£11.65
11–15	£12.65
16 and over	£13.65

The amount you get is *half* the amount by which your actual income falls short of the income limits set out above. For example, a family with two children under 11 can benefit if their income does not exceed £110.25 (i.e. £98.60 plus £11.65). If the family's actual income is £90.25, they are £20 short of the limit so FIS will pay them half of this – £10 a week.

There is a limit to the amount of money you can get out of FIS, however. These ceilings came into force in July 1986:

	Maximum FIS
for a one-child family where the child is:	
under 11	£25.30
11–15	£25.80
16 and over	£26.30
increase for each additional child	
under 11	£2.55
11–15	£3.05
16 and over	£3.55

Supplementary Benefit

This is a weekly cash payment, tax free to most people, though strictly it is taxable if you are claiming the benefit because you are unemployed. Most claimants find the benefit is below their starting point for tax anyway – and in any case, a single parent with a child under 16 does not have to register for work to be able to claim Supplementary Benefit.

The amount you get depends on your circumstances and on your income, if any. The bigger your outgoings – heating, lighting, feeding and clothing yourself and your children, etc. – the larger the amount it's reckoned you need to live on. The Department of Health and Social Security has its own ideas of how much everyone needs. These are called 'scale rates'. If your income falls short of your scale rate, Supplementary Benefit makes up the difference.

The first £4 a week of any earnings you have are

ignored. If you are a single parent, then half of the next £16 of earnings is also ignored. In other words, receiving these comparatively small sums *won't* lead to a cut in your benefit.

However, if you have substantial savings – and anything over £3,000 counts as substantial – then you'll be expected to live on this money until your savings fall below £3,000; you won't be given Supplementary Benefit. Rules that used to treat life policies as savings that could be cashed in for living expenses have been relaxed in recent years.

Amounts of benefit differ according to personal circumstances, but broadly speaking the rate (from July 1986) for a single householder is £29.80 a week, plus £10.20 for a dependant under 11, £15.30 for a dependant aged 11–15, £18.40 for a dependant of 16 or 17, and £23.85 if you have a dependent child over 18.

After a year, you go onto the long-term rate of benefit, which is still hardly riches but is a good bit better than the starting rate, paying £37.90 for a single householder.

If you qualify for Supplementary Benefit, you can apply for one-off payments for things like furniture and a cooker – very useful if your marriage has broken up in circumstances that have left you effectively homeless. However, if you have savings of more than £500 it's likely you'll be expected to spend your own money before making a claim. And in addition, the government plans to phase out many one-off payments on the basis that most Supplementary Benefit claimants should be able to save for such items from their benefit.

A word of warning!

☞ If you are considering claiming maintenance from your husband or ex-husband, and he is himself on a very low income, you may well be better off claiming Supplementary Benefit – it could be more reliable, and there are spin-off benefits too.

The hidden benefits of FIS and SB
When you claim Family Income Supplement or Supple-

mentary Benefit you also qualify automatically for a list
of other useful benefits, such as:

£   free milk and vitamins for children under 5

£   free school meals for your children

£   free prescriptions

£   free dental treatment

£   free spectacles

£   free legal help, using the Green Form scheme.

Housing Benefit

Housing Benefit is a cash allowance paid by the local
authority. You don't need any qualifying number of
national insurance contributions, but the allowance is
means-tested: what you get depends on the size of your
income compared with your rent and rates.

If you qualify for Supplementary Benefit you will get
Housing Benefit too. Even if your income is a bit too
high for Supplementary Benefit, you may still be able to
meet the limits for Housing Benefit, which are a bit
more generous.

If you don't receive Supplementary Benefit, apply
direct to the council for Housing Benefit. They will set
your benefit entitlement against rates due to them –
and if you're a council tenant the benefit will also go
towards your rent. If you are a tenant of a private
landlord you will be sent a rent cheque to enable you to
pay your rent.

State Pensions for Divorcees

If you are involved in a legal tussle over things like
access to children, how much you want – or are pre-
pared to pay – in maintenance, the future of the family
home, etc., then these day-to-day problems can push
long-term issues further and further into the back-

ground. It is a mistake to let this happen, even if it is understandable.

Divorce is as permanent a step as marriage and there is no reason to think that you will necessarily marry again, or that your former spouse will make a return trip down the aisle. Think ahead to what you will live on when you reach retirement age.

Entitlement to a state pension depends on having paid – or been credited with – a certain number of national insurance contributions. To get any basic pension at all you must actually have paid sufficient NI contributions in any one tax year since 1975 for that to count as a 'qualifying' year, *or* you must have paid 50 flat-rate contributions before 6 April 1975.

To receive the full rate of basic pension, about nine-tenths of the years of your working life must count as qualifying years, with contributions either paid or credited.

In most cases, a husband's state pension will not be affected by separation or divorce. If he is working, he will carry on making national insurance contributions, which will eventually bring a pension at the full rate when he is 65. Even if he is unemployed, his contributions will be credited so his pension rights are preserved.

A wife or ex-wife may not be in such a happy position. A married woman can go the whole of her life without paying a national insurance contribution, either because she is not working or, if she is, because her earnings are so low they are below the national insurance threshold.

And even if she has been working in a job with a decent wage, she may well have opted (before April 1978, when this choice was withdrawn for anyone who had not already made it) to pay the reduced rate of contributions – the so-called 'married woman's stamp' – which, while it does count for some benefits, does not earn a state pension. As long as she is married, none of this matters. Her husband's contributions will pay for a state pension at the married man's rate, and if she survives him she will be paid a widow's pension.

But if a woman is divorced, her position is more

complex. She can start making national insurance contributions herself (and if she is working and earning over the NI threshold then she'll have no choice in the matter), which will count towards a pension. And, for the years up to and including the one in which the marriage ended, she can make her ex-husband's contributions count towards her pension if his NI record for those years was better than hers. Her pension will be paid to her when she reaches 60, if she then retires – she does not have to wait for her ex-husband to retire, in contrast with married women, who are not paid a pension until their husband draws his.

Wives who are separated from their husbands rather than actually divorced do not have this problem. DHSS rules treat them as still dependent on their husband, so a woman can live apart from her husband for decades, never pay a single national insurance contribution, and yet still be able to claim a pension based on what her husband has paid in! There are two snags, however:

* she can't claim her pension until her husband retires – if he is younger than her this can be very inconvenient;

* when she gets her pension, it will *not* be at the single person's rate – she will get the difference between a single man's pension and a married man's pension, currently £23.25 a week (from July 1986).

Women who are already over 60 when they are divorced also escape the worst effects of divorce on their pension rights. Like any other wife, they can claim a state pension based on their own NI payments if they have made enough, but this is only any help in a minority of instances. Not to worry though, because a woman over 60 has already reached pensionable age and can make a claim based on her ex-husband's contributions for the years up to the end of the financial year in which she had her 59th birthday.

Using your ex's contributions
If you think you may get a better pension by relying on

your ex-spouse's NI payments, allow time for his or her records to be traced and checked. Do not present yourself at the enquiry counter of a DHSS office on the day you reach retirement age and expect to walk out with a cheque.

The social security office should contact you about four months before you reach retirement age; allow a month after this and, if they've not been in touch, you contact them and start the ball rolling – or you won't get your pension on time.

Re-marriage

A divorced woman who re-marries before she reaches 60 loses all rights to a state pension based on her ex-husband's national insurance record. She has to rely on her own contributions and those of her new husband. It may not be the most diplomatic topic to raise, but ex-wives considering a second go at marriage in the autumn of their years might like to work into a conversation with their intended the subject of how complete his NI payments have been!

Ex-husbands

The pension rules do have an element of sexual equality in them, unlike some other aspects of divorce law. In the unlikely event that her NI record is better than his, an ex-husband can claim a state pension based on his former wife's national insurance contributions during the years they were married. However, if he re-marries before reaching retirement age he gives up this right.

Widows

A widow is the surviving wife of a man who has died, but if there has been a divorce then the ex-wife does not count as a widow and is *not* entitled to widows' benefits and allowances. On the other hand, separation does not end a marriage. If a couple are merely separated, then when the husband dies the wife *will* become a widow and *will* be able to claim benefits – assuming her husband has made the required number of national insurance contributions.

National Insurance when Your Marriage Breaks Down

Many wives face a bit of a shock in relation to their national insurance payments when their marriage ends, either because they have just started work for the first time in years and find the rates nowadays are much higher than they remember, or because they have been working but paying the reduced rate 'married woman's stamp'. As the name implies though, this is only for married women – get a divorce and you don't qualify.

Until 1978 wives could elect to pay NI contributions at a much reduced rate. Their payments didn't earn the full range of benefits, but most women felt they could rely on their husband's contributions for what they wanted. In April 1978 the right to choose to pay at the married woman's rate was scrapped, though wives already paying at the lower rate have been allowed to carry on doing so.

A working woman paying contributions at the lower rate must tell her employer as soon as the decree absolute is granted. From that date, she is a single person under DHSS rules and must pay full NI contributions. She should also ask her boss to give her back the certificate showing she has been liable only at the lower rate; the certificate is not valid any longer and the ex-wife has to return it to her social security office, telling them she no longer qualifies.

All ex-wives, then, whether they have worked before their divorce or are just starting work for the first time in recent years, will find they now have to pay into the national insurance scheme at the full rate if their earnings are above the NI threshold, which is currently £38.00 a week (from 6 April 1986).

Once you earn over the £38 threshold, national insurance contributions are due on *all* your earnings, not just the excess over £38. You pay nothing extra once your earnings top £285 a week. This is the full contributions scale at the moment (1986–87) for workers who are

not contracted out of the State Earnings Related Pension
Scheme:

Gross weekly pay	Employee's NI rate
£38.00–59.99	5%
£60.00–94.99	7%
£95.00–139.99	9%
£140.00–285.00	9%
over £285	NIL

If you are self-employed you pay a flat-rate contribution of £3.75 a week plus a separate Class 4 contribution,
which in 1986–87 is 6.3 per cent of your business profits
between £4,450 and £14,820 per year.

Home Responsibilities Protection
Suppose you are a divorced mother, unable to get a full-
time job because of looking after your children, and
therefore unable to contribute towards your own state
pension? Does this mean you have a pensionless retirement ahead of you? The answer is no, though this
doesn't mean the problem has disappeared altogether.

In 1978 the Home Responsibilities scheme (HRP)
was introduced to make it easier for people to earn a
state pension even if they have to stay at home for part
of their working life to look after children or someone
who is elderly, or an invalid. HRP does this by cutting
the number of years you have to pay national insurance
in order to qualify for a pension.

The scheme is being phased in, but broadly speaking
it means that instead of having to work, and pay NI
contributions, for about 40 years to qualify for a pension, this can be cut to around 20 years without losing a
penny when you retire.

You get HRP automatically if you are receiving Child
Benefit for a child under 16, or if you are receiving
Supplementary Benefit *and* you are unable to go out to
work because you are looking after an elderly or sick
person at home. Not unnaturally, you can't have HRP,
which gives the benefits of full NI payments, and at
the same time have the right to pay the reduced-rate

married woman's contribution – though this won't affect anyone who is already divorced.

Most people who benefit from HRP are women, but the scheme does cover men too. Not many men will qualify because of the way our social security system casts men in the role of breadwinners and women in the role of dependants. Men who think they may qualify – perhaps because they are living with a woman who is effectively supporting them – should apply to the local DHSS office. If the basis of the claim is that they can't work because they are looking after children, it is likely the right to Child Benefit will have to be formally transferred to the father from the children's mother, if this hasn't already been done.

=====

Job Pensions: The Widow's Mite or the Widow's Might?
Job pensions and divorce do not mix. Pension rights are often an individual's most valuable asset – yet the money can't be touched before retirement and it is virtually impossible to divide it, either by agreement or by court order.

In a normal marriage, wives can expect two separate benefits from their husband's occupational pension scheme:

£   if the husband dies before retiring, the widow should get a lump sum plus a pension;

£   if he dies after retiring and drawing the job pension himself for some time, his widow will get a pension for the rest of her life.

Divorce ends both these expectations. As things are at the moment, a widow's pension can be paid only to a widow. An ex-wife is totally at the mercy of the pension fund trustees. Some do make voluntary payments, particularly to young ex-wives with children; but this cannot be relied upon.

This means that a wife of 30 years, say, can spend her life as a homebuilder, be divorced when it is too late for her to make a career of her own, then see her ex-husband drop dead a month later without leaving her a penny in pension benefits from his employer – even if the husband had been perfectly willing to do so.

The obvious answer is for any wife involved in a divorce to demand that as part of the financial settlement her husband should make alternative pension arrangements to cover her. This is ideal – but it is also prohibitively expensive for almost every husband. Very few can even dream of slapping down many thousands of pounds in a lump sum to buy their ex-wife the promise of a pension that will match the one provided by a job scheme the husband might have spent decades paying into.

The Lord Chancellor's answer

In July 1985 the Lord Chancellor, Lord Hailsham, issued a discussion paper, *Occupational Pension Rights on Divorce*, proposing changes in the law to give ex-wives the right to a slice of their husband's job pension (or, for that matter, allowing ex-husbands to claim against their wife's pension). The planned changes would give a woman the right to ask the court at the time of her divorce for permission to apply *later* for some or all of any widow's pension due when her husband dies. The court might refuse, saying the overall financial settlement was already enough, or that the wife had good pension prospects of her own.

If the court did give the go-ahead, no figure would be fixed; this would be left until the husband had actually died, when the former wife would have six months to go back to court and ask to be awarded a portion of his pension. And at this stage the real widow – the woman married to the man at the time of his death – would also be forced to join in the legal battle over his pension if she wanted to be sure of telling her side of the story before it was too late.

The clear implication of this is that second or subsequent wives could well find themselves with a pittance of a widow's pension because the bulk of the cash might go to an earlier wife. And there will be no way of telling just what will happen until it's too late to do anything about it!

Ladies considering marrying divorced men might in future have to make careful enquiries about their financial well-being in the event of their husband's death.

The proposals will add nothing to the size of the pension money available. If made law, they will simply divide the one widow's pension between all the wives and ex-wives on the scene, however many there are. Whatever the logic in the proposals, and however unfair the results of the present system can be, the prospects for undignified squabbling in the weeks following a man's death are unappealing in the extreme and it seems certain that many women will give up their rights rather than press their claim.

Under the present law, if a husband wants to benefit a particular dependant or dependants, he should make sure the trustees of his employer's pension fund are aware of his wishes. They don't have to follow them, but they often do if the fund's rules let them.

And a wife who is about to become an ex-wife, while almost powerless under the present system, should find out precisely what she's losing and give serious thought to at least insuring her ex-husband's life for as much as she can afford – perhaps even getting him to take the premiums into account as part of the maintenance settlement. This will give her some legitimate profit on his demise.

9

Take Cover! –
Insurance after the
Breakdown

So now you are divorced, it's time to think about insurance. Former wives face three worries:

- What happens if their ex-husband dies?

- What happens if he falls ill and can't keep up the maintenance payments?

- Will it be possible to make ends meet if he goes back to the court and wins a reduction in the payments?

Husbands may say that the first two of these circumstances are hardly their worry – and it is difficult to contradict someone who takes the attitude that, if he's dead, well then he certainly isn't going to be worrying about how his former wife is faring at the check-out at Sainsbury's. They are, if you like, moral responsibilities. However, men certainly do lose some sleep whenever their ex-wife threatens to ask for an increase in payments, and this is something an insurance policy can protect against.

There are, then, three types of insurance that are helpful to former husbands and wives in the wake of a divorce:

- life insurance

- health insurance

- cover against a change in the amount of maintenance due.

Life Insurance

Almost without exception, court orders for maintenance die along with the payer. Few ex-husbands are so wealthy that they can set aside investments that are big enough to generate the same amount in dividends and interest as they have been paying in maintenance.

Ex-wives, particularly those with young children, should insure the life of their former spouse for as much as they can afford. There are two ways to do this cheaply:

* A **whole life policy** – that is, a policy that lasts for the whole of the ex-husband's life and pays out only when he dies. NB – this means that, unlike an endowment policy, there is no sum paid after 10 years, or 20 years, or whatever.

* A **term policy,** which lasts for a set number of years – for example, until the children have reached a particular age and the former wife can find a job. Like whole life policies, term policies pay out only if the ex-husband dies within the term of the policy – they are not savings policies and there is no benefit unless the insured dies.

Normally insurance policies pay a lump sum when the person insured dies, but some schemes offer regular payments instead. Wives who like the idea of a regular payment (at least while the policy runs) to replace their lost maintenance – or who don't like the responsibility of investing a lump sum – should ask any insurance broker about these family income benefit schemes.

A bit less obvious . . .
It's pretty clear why ex-wives should insure ex-husbands, but there's at least one good reason why many ex-husbands should also take out a policy on the life of their former wife: children.

Assuming the wife looks after the children when the marriage breaks down, who would look after them if the wife fell under a bus? Either the husband would have to give up his job to look after them, or he would have to rearrange his domestic life, perhaps bringing in a housekeeper or relative to help. Either way involves expense, and that's why fathers should take a look at life insurance too.

In Sickness and in Health

Marriage may be for better or for worse, in sickness and in health, so why should divorce be any different! It's not the most important thing to bear in mind when you're going through the divorce mill, but ill-health can often have financial side effects – like making a husband less able to afford the monthly maintenance cheque. Permanent health insurance can provide a safety net.

Premium levels vary enormously, depending on age, occupation and how much you expect to be able to claim, so do shop around by using an insurance broker.

Guarding against a New Order

The idea of a clean break is fine in principle. What often happens in practice is that money matters mean a couple spend the rest of their lives in each other's pockets (or purses, or wallets . . .), because every time one of them undergoes a change in circumstances it's a case of going back to the courts for a return match.

Now, though, you can at least insure against losing. It is possible to obtain a policy that will insure you against being told to pay more – or, if you're on the other side, against having to make do with less.

The conditions are pretty strict, however. Policies are meant to guard against the unforeseen – like a man being made redundant, or losing his business through bankruptcy. So a former wife can't insure against a fall in her maintenance just because her ex-husband is about to retire at 65! If the marriage had survived, her income would presumably have fallen anyway.

Similarly, a former husband can take out a policy that would pay up if he were ordered to pay increased maintenance because his ex-wife fell ill and could no longer work. But he can't insure against being told to pay more because he himself has had the good fortune to receive a salary increase!

10

Will Power

Marriage, separation and divorce can do funny things to your will – and not always the funny things you might expect.

Marriage

When you get married your existing will is automatically cancelled. If you die without having made out a new one, you die intestate – which means that whatever you leave is divided under rules set out in the intestacy laws.

Basically, the rules give a surviving spouse the first £40,000 of your estate. He or she also gets the income from half of any balance – but not the capital itself. The rest goes to your children.

If this isn't what you want, make out a new will when you wed. If you think writing a will while you're on your honeymoon is more than a bit morbid (which it is), there's a loophole. You are allowed to make out a will before you get married *as long as you make clear in the will that it is being made with the forthcoming marriage in mind*. A will like this – the lawyers call it a will 'made in contemplation of marriage' – is not cancelled as soon as you sign the marriage register.

Separation

Merely separating has no effect whatsoever on your will. If you make out a will leaving everything to your husband or wife, you could then live at opposite ends of the country for the next 20 years, hating every fibre of each other's being – but your will, made before the rot set in, would carry on regardless. On your death, the hated one would get the lot!

Moral!

 If you've got anything worth leaving, leave it to someone worth loving; make out a new will as soon as you separate.

Divorce

Divorce does have an effect on your will – and what an effect! Saloon bar mythology has it that divorce makes your will void, just like marriage. There is a lot of logic in this, so it's a pity that it's wrong.

Divorce does two things:

* it cancels any instructions that named the spouse as your executor or executrix;

* it strips out of the will any bequests you made to your spouse.

As with a will written just before marriage, you can – if you wish – get round this by saying quite clearly in your will that the bequest should go ahead even if you are no longer married to the beneficiary at the time of your death.

But if you don't say that – and how many people do! – then the results can be very odd.

Suppose, for example, a husband was worth £20,000. And suppose he made a will leaving £19,900 to his wife and the residue of his estate to his pals at the Goat and Compasses for a farewell drink. And suppose then that he got divorced . . .

The upshot would be that the wife's bequest would be scrapped, and there'd be a £20,000 booze-up at the Goat and Compasses!

Remember!

☞ Divorce does not cancel your will. It just makes it rather lopsided! Make a new one as soon as you can.

So the mean old so-and-so has cut you off without a penny . . .

Being left out of a former spouse's will — or cut out of it because of the rule cancelling bequests on divorce — might, you would think, be the end of the story. But it isn't.

An ex-wife, or an ex-husband for that matter, has six months from the time probate is granted in which to lodge a claim for a slice of the estate, as long as they have not themselves re-married. For obvious reasons, most claims come from ex-wives who object to the fact that their former husband has left everything to his second wife.

The ex-wife should try to convince the court that she will suffer financial hardship by being left out of the will. The court will then take the following points into account:

* the ex-wife's finances;

* the financial circumstances of beneficiaries under the will;

* the amount left by the deceased;

* the terms of the divorce settlement.

This last point can be the rock that will sink many claims, particularly since the 'clean break' became the aim in divorce cases. After all, you can't say it's a clean break if one party can come back years later and raid the other's estate!

HEADING OFF A RAID IN ADVANCE

Men who are planning to re-marry, or who just want to make sure their money goes where they want it to go, can act in advance to stop an ex-wife's attack on their estate. At the time of their divorce they should ask the court to order, as part of the overall financial settlement, that the wife is barred from making any claim against their estate.

THE WIFE'S ANSWER

If you are a wife going through the divorce process and your husband comes up with a demand that you be stopped from making a claim against his estate, there are at least three answers open to you:

* you can roll over and say yes;

* you can tell the court the overall financial proposals still leave you dependent on your husband so it would be unjust to ban a claim;

* you can agree to the ban – on condition the husband takes out a sizeable life insurance policy with you as the beneficiary, so you will, in fact, benefit on his death.

Remember!

☞ The court can grant the husband's request for a ban even if you don't agree, so don't shrug off all thought of negotiation. Half an estate is better than no estate at all.

A MESSAGE FROM BEYOND

A clean break used to be something that happened to your leg on a rugby field. Former husbands who were divorced before the great fuss about abolishing a meal ticket for life may now be horrified at the thought that, having paid out handsomely to get rid of wife number one, she may re-emerge to fight wife number two for the spoils.

If you are in this position and think you've paid enough, there is something you can do. When you make your will leaving everything to wife number two (or to a cats' home, or to pay off the National Debt, or whatever you like), write a letter at the same time. Explain that you haven't left out your first wife simply because she slipped your mind. Then say just why you have left her out!

This isn't a *guaranteed* winner, because the court can do what it likes with your will; that's the law. But your message from the other side will be accepted as evidence in just the same way as are the financial statements from the claimant and other potential beneficiaries.

North of the Border

In Scotland a will is *not* affected by divorce, and the intestacy rules are slightly different too. The surviving spouse gets the family home if it's worth under £50,000 – or £50,000 in cash if it is worth more – plus domestic effects worth up to £10,000 in all. He or she also takes the next £15,000 from the estate, together with a one-third share of the balance. The remainder is divided between the children.

11

Without Benefit of Clergy

If splitting up is so easy – leaving aside the possible financial complications – then why get married in the first place? It's a good question, because the fact is that our cock-eyed tax system means millions of couples would be better off never going near a vicar or a registrar.

Tax

In an ordinary married couple the husband gets the married man's tax allowance of £3,655 (1986-87) and the wife is allowed to earn £2,335 before starting to pay tax. Any investment income she has, such as savings bank interest, is taxed in her husband's name – she can't use her tax allowance against it.

The couple get no tax allowance for having children. This was abolished in 1977 when Child Benefit was made tax free. They do get tax relief on one mortgage of up to £30,000, but if this, plus their other tax reliefs, still leaves them well off, then their incomes are added together by the tax man so they reach the higher rate tax bands twice as fast as two single people.

They can avoid this by asking to be taxed as if they still were single people – but if they do, the husband loses his married man's allowance, and the wife's investment income is *still* taxed in his name.

They can have one residence which is exempt from capital gains tax when they sell it. If they have other property or investments, and sell them at a profit, they pay tax at 30 per cent as soon as their annual taxable gains top £6,300.

They can switch investments between each other without incurring capital gains tax.

But if they weren't married . . .'
The same couple, but assuming they were not married, would be treated quite differently.

£   They would both get the single person's tax allowance.

£   Any investment income the woman received would be taxed as her own, and she could use her tax allowance to cut the tax due.

£   If they had children they would get the single parent's Additional Personal Allowance – and by claiming for one child each, they could get two allowances. Their Child Benefit would not be affected.

£   Their income would not be added together by the tax inspector, so they would reach the higher rate tax bands much more slowly than if they were wed.

£   They could each claim tax relief on a mortgage of up to £30,000 – even if the two mortgages are on one home, as long as there really are two loans.

£   If one partner does not have enough income to use up his or her tax allowances, well that's no problem. The other partner can make out a deed of covenant transferring enough income to absorb the spare reliefs and get the poorer partner a pleasant tax refund cheque.

£   If they have two homes, one partner can claim the gains tax exemption for one and the other partner can claim for the second home, so they effectively get a tax-free investment property – probably bought with that extra £30,000 mortgage! If they do have other investments that produce gains on which tax might be due, they are each allowed £6,300 a year tax free.

The pro's and con's

Married	Unmarried
• husband's tax threshold £3,655	• man's tax threshold £2,335
• wife's tax threshold £2,335 – but she only gets this allowance against her earned income	• woman's tax threshold £2,335 – allowable against any income, earned or from investments
• no tax allowance for children	• can claim £1,320 tax allowance (double if each partner claims for one child)
• can claim Child Benefit	• can claim Child Benefit
• can claim tax relief on mortgage up to £30,000	• can claim tax relief on two mortgages up to £30,000 each
• start paying higher rate tax when *combined* income after tax allowances tops £17,200	• start paying higher rate tax when *individual* income after tax allowances tops £17,200
• income covenanted from one spouse to the other has no tax effect	• covenant can be used to shift income from one partner to the other to minimise tax or obtain a refund
• couple can have only one residence exempt from gains tax	• couple can have two residences exempt from gains tax
• couple can make £6,300 a year investment profits free of gains tax	• couple can make £6,300 a year *each* in investment profits free of gains tax
• bequests from one partner to the other are exempt from inheritance tax	• bequests may be taxable – but only if the donor leaves a substantial estate overall

Affiliation Orders

There is one further massive advantage a couple can claim if they are unmarried parents. They can go to court, where the man can consent to an affiliation order under which he will pay for the support of his child until it grows up. These payments count for tax relief, so, for example, a father who pays tax at the basic 29 per cent rate would save £290 in tax for every £1,000 paid out under an affiliation order.

In effect, this means the unmarried couple are getting tax relief on the cost of raising their child, from birth right through to the time the child finishes its education – something Parliament deliberately abolished for ordinary married couples.

Living Apart after Living Together

About 1 million people in this country are living with someone in a stable relationship but without being legally married. And almost a quarter of all married couples aged 16–34 did live together before they wed. So, while you can't get divorced if you are single, being single doesn't always cut you off from potentially major disputes over property and money.

While the romance lasts, couples should steel themselves to make a binding agreement over who owns what in their partnership. Sometimes this will be obvious: the partner who owned the Jaguar XJ6 before the couple got together will still own it after the relationship has ended.

The real problems arise over assets like a house or a flat that are purchased with contributions from both partners, and over major items that one partner claims were a gift but the other partner declares were simply a loan.

Property

In property disputes, what seems to count most is the name on the title deeds. If your name isn't on the deeds when you and your partner part, don't think a court will give you a slice of your home simply because you looked after the children, or because your need for the property is more urgent than your ex-partner's. These things count when you are wed – but not when you aren't.

To prove a claim, you must show you put money into the property, either for its purchase or for maintenance or improvement. Time spent in work on the property can also count. The real clincher is proof that when the property was bought it was intended that you should have a legal stake in it. If you're on the receiving end of a deal like this, try to get your loved one to put it in writing!

When is a gift not a gift?

Goods bought by one partner for the other can create similar problems. How do you prove a gift is really a gift and not merely a loan?

In one recent case a divorcee presented her boyfriend with a £5,000 car on Christmas Day, having sprayed the words 'Merry Christmas' in foam on the windscreen. When they later fell out she snatched the car back and he promptly sued her for it. She won, after claiming she had only intended to give the boyfriend the *use* of the car, and not the car itself – though in a Judgement of Solomon, the boyfriend was told that as he'd put a lot of work into the vehicle he could keep it if he gave the divorcee just over £2,000!

Joint ownership

Items bought jointly can also create a legal tangle. They are held on what the lawyers call a 'trust for sale', which means either of the joint owners can insist on the sale of the item and the division of the proceeds. In practice, of course, it may take legal action to get the desired result – assuming the court agrees the goods in question are actually jointly owned in the first place and not the exclusive property of just one partner.

Things to come

The Law Commission, which gives advice to the government on legal reforms, has studied the question of how unmarried partners can be given firm rights to a share of their home, in roughly the same way that a wife can almost automatically claim a share in the matrimonial home even if her name is not on the deeds.

However, even if the Commission comes down in favour of endowing unmarried people with some of the rights granted to those who have legalised their relationship, and even if Parliament accepts the idea, it will almost certainly be a year or two before such changes can be made. Until then, anyone living with another person outside marriage should keep as detailed a record as possible of who bought what, and who contributed how much towards major items. It's not romantic, but it is common sense.

Scotland the brave

England may be about to give live-in lovers legal rights, over 200 years after abolishing common-law marriages. Scotland, by being courageous enough never to abolish common-law marriage in the first place, has seen the issue turn full circle.

In Scotland it is still possible to be married without any form of ceremony – it's called **marriage by cohabitation with habit and repute.** This doesn't mean that a one night stand anywhere north of Carlisle will leave you hitched for life next morning. But a lengthy and stable relationship in which both partners regard themselves as married, and outsiders do too, can result in marriage.

Maintenance

Unmarried couples have no obligation to maintain one another, either during or after their relationship. If there are children, though, both parents have a continuing responsibility for their support. Typically, this means that when the couple split up the mother will apply for an order against the father – though she will get maintenance only for the children, not for herself as well.

If you want the rights – and the risks – of matrimony, you still have to go through the legal hoops of getting married to get them.

Remember!

☞ If you don't get married, you miss all the excitement of getting divorced.

Further Reading for Your Spare Time

If you want to read even more on the financial consequences of divorce and separation, and the other topics, such as legal aid, touched on in this book, there is no shortage of material available. Happily, much of it comes completely free. All the literature listed here is free of charge unless a price is stated.

Undefended Divorce. From county courts or by post from The Lord Chancellor's Department, Neville House, Page Street, London SW1.

Maintenance Payments Plan. Pamphlet and application form covering insurance against amendments to a maintenance order: Partnership Services (Maintenance) Ltd, Ludgate House, 107 Fleet Street, London EC4.

Ancillary Relief & Family Provision. Booklet about the FLBA conciliation scheme: Family Law Bar Association Conciliation Board, 2 Harcourt Buildings, Temple, London EC4.

List of local solicitors with a special interest in matri-
monial matters: Secretary, Solicitors' Family Law
Association, Messrs Speechly Bircham, 154 Fleet
Street, London EC4.

The Divorce Book. Particularly good advice for separating parents on how to explain the break-up to their
children. Price 95p plus 20p postage: National
Marriage Guidance Council, Herbert Gray College,
Little Church Street, Rugby, Warwickshire.

Divorce and Tax – A Straightforward Guide. Simple booklet on tax problems arising from marriage breakdown: Messrs Bazley White & Co. (Solicitors),
8 Portman Street, London W1.

Income Tax and Married Couples – pamphlet IR31
Income Tax: Separation and Divorce – pamphlet IR30
Income Tax and One-Parent Families – pamphlet IR29.
All available from any tax inspector's office – look in
the telephone book under 'Inland Revenue' for your
nearest branch.

Financial Aspects of Separation and Divorce. Booklet
offering succinct tips on tax, maintenance, wills,
property, etc. Price £1 from Messrs Neville Russell
(Chartered Accountants), 246 Bishopsgate, London
EC2.

PROMISE – Programmed Monthly Income Service.
Pamphlet describing investment schemes for
divorcees who want to invest a lump sum to produce
regular income: Richard Neville Financial Manage-
ment, 10 Copthall Avenue, London EC2.

Getting Legal Help! Leaflet explaining what legal aid
covers and how you can get it: available from courts,
law centres, Citizens' Advice Bureaux, etc., or from
The Law Society, 113 Chancery Lane, London WC2.

Legal Aid – Financial Limits. Leaflet describing the income and capital you can have while qualifying for

the legal aid and the legal advice and assistance schemes: from courts, etc., or from Legal Aid Head Office, Newspaper House, 8 Great New Street, London EC4.

Legal Aid – the Statutory Charge. Leaflet describing how cash or property awarded by a court can be taken in repayment of legal aid you have received: from courts, etc., or from the Law Society, 113 Chancery Lane, London WC2.

Your Retirement Pension – pamphlet NP32.
Retirement Benefits for Married Women – pamphlet NP32B.
Your Retirement Pension if you are Widowed or Divorced – pamphlet NP32A.
One Parent Benefit – pamphlet CH11.
Cash Help – pamphlet SB1, describes supplementary benefit.
Family Income Supplement – pamphlet FIS1.
Help for One-Parent Families – pamphlet FB3.
Child's Special Allowance – pamphlet NI93.
Who Pays Less Rent and Rates? – pamphlet RR1.
All the above pamphlets are available at local social security offices, or by post from DHSS Leaflets Unit, PO Box 21, Stanmore, Middlesex HA7 1AY.

Finding Help

Finding someone to talk to who has, perhaps, been through a broken marriage and can speak from experience can be a lot more useful than reading about it all in theory. These organisations can all help with some aspect or another of problems arising from separation and divorce.

Who they are	*Who they cater for*
National Marriage Guidance Council, Herbert Gray College, Little Church Street, Rugby, Warwickshire	Anyone with a marriage problem – even if they're not planning to divorce. Couples can seek advice together or as individuals. Local addresses in your phone directory.
Gingerbread, 35 Wellington Street, London WC2	Single parents, via Gingerbread groups.
Scottish Council for Single Parents in Scotland, 13 Gayfield Square, Edinburgh EH1 3NX	As the name says, single parents north of the border.

National Council for One Parent Families, 255 Kentish Town Road, London NW5	Single parents needing advice.
Citizens' Advice Bureaux	Almost anyone needing advice or help with legal or financial problems; national network – addresses in your local phone book.
Law Centres' Federation, Duchess House, Warren Street, London NW1	People seeking their nearest free law centre as they can't afford a solicitor.
Catholic Marriage Advisory Council, 15 Lansdowne Road, London W11	People – including non-Catholics – wanting counselling over marriage problems.
Jewish Marriage Council, 23 Ravenshurst Avenue, London NW4	Jewish people – single or married – needing advice over personal relationships.

Index